What Sistas are saying about Totally Devoted 3

God calls some people to preach His word, some to sing His praises, some to teach His Word, and others to simply be a witness to others. There is no doubt that God has called Polly to write devotions to encourage, inspire, and bless "the socks off" her sistas. With each devotion that I read and study, I find myself asking, "How did she know that I was feeling like that?" In her Totally Devoted 3, she truly identifies with the inward thoughts, feelings, and struggles that we as daughters, wives, mothers, and sistas often experience but may not admit to others. Through her scripture based devotions written for women "on the go," she reminds us that with God all things are possible, that God never fails, and that God understands, forgives, and treasures all of us sistas.

Tammy Castleberry
Principal, Macedonia Elementary
Canton, GA

Polly's insightful, Holy Spirit-inspired devotions bring great encouragement to the Body of Christ. They are packed with God-honoring truth that helps us "not to grow weary in well doing." A great read to start or end your day.

Deborah Rey
Volunteer Coordinator, The HOPE Center
Woodstock, GA

Polly truly knows the heart of a woman in writing her Daily Devotions for "Totally Devoted." I became hooked after the first one and felt that she was giving me insight into passages I thought I already knew, along with reading good personal stories. They are full of rich scripture and insight and I recommend any woman with a heart to become more Christ-like.

Karen Covell
Founding Director, Hollywood Prayer Network
Hollywood, CA

I have worked with Polly Balint in her role as journalist and writer for more than 20 years and I am always impressed by her ability to get to the heart of the matter when she tackles any subject. Where she really shines is when she combines her gift as a spiritual leader with her talent as a writer to shine a direct light on what it takes to live as a Christian in today's world.

Rebecca Johnston
Managing Editor, Cherokee Tribune,
Canton, GA

I just finished reading your devotions. These are great! Practical applications and helpful insights illustrated by your own willingness to be transparent about your own heart struggles. We all need (especially women!) encouragement to go to the Lord and identify the lies Satan tries to use to obtain strongholds in our lives. The world is a crazy mixed up place, constantly bombarding us with half truths and opinions rather than the source of truth and peace that can only be found by returning to the Word and to the foot of the cross. You do a great job of reminding us to hear the Lord's voice above the maddening crowd. I would love to recommend and want to read your other devotional books. You go, Girl!!

Beth Stull
B.C.C.L.C./Office Manager
Access Strategies, Inc.
Cumming, GA

I have been under Polly's teaching and leadership previously and I can tell you that Polly is passionate about her relationship with the Lord. Polly's devotion is contagious and her writings are relevant, convicting, encouraging and chock-full of refreshing scripture which I love! Every woman in every season can benefit from Polly's passion and devotionals.

Dana Banister Coleman
REALTOR
Harry Norman Realtors
Metro Atlanta, GA

totally

devoted 3

by Polly Balint

Totally Devoted 3, a devotional book by Polly Balint, Founder & President of That Girl Marketing, LLC

Edited by Grace Balint

Back Cover Photo by Kam Roberts of One Girl Photography
Front Cover Graphics by Jjinc Designs

Published by Yawn's Publishing
198 North Street
Canton, GA 30114
www.yawnsbooks.com

ISBN: 978-1-940395-05-0

Library of Congress Control Number: 2013948037

Printed in the United States

All Scripture quoted will be from the NIV translation unless otherwise noted.

Consider inviting Polly to speak at your next women's event!
Contact her @:

Polly Balint
That Girl Marketing, LLC
~~**www.thatgirlmarketing.biz**~~
~~**polly@thatgirlmarketing.biz**~~
www.facebook.com/thatpollybalint
https://twitter.com/pollyisthatgirl

With a very thankful heart...

This is the hardest part of writing a book, because I don't want to leave anyone out when I give thanks. I have *so* much to be thankful for, and so many people to thank, that it will take another book to acknowledge all the people who have helped me with their godly insight and wisdom, prayed for me, encouraged me with a hug, a note and a smile.

First of all, I thank God for giving me life and, through the blood of Jesus Christ, I have life in abundance! Thank you, Lord, for inspiring me to write this book and helping me every step of the way. May Your Name be richly glorified every time this book is read.

I thank the LORD for you, Don, my precious husband and best friend, my intimate companion, my personal Bible scholar and mentor, and the godly father of our lovely daughters. You walk in wisdom and humility. Thank you for loving me, helping me and encouraging me in countless ways. I love you deeply and I'm so grateful to God that I get to be your wife.

Grace and Mary, you are true gifts to your mother's heart and you both inspire me with your passions for God, His word, for love and for living abundant lives in Jesus! You encourage me with your love and prayers. I learn so much when I am drawing on your 20-somethings' insight into the world we are living in. Thank you! My love and hugs and kisses to you both because you are dearly loved and appreciated!

And Grace, as my new editor, thank you for your expertise and your wise and patient editing with this manuscript. Thank you for the smiley faces and happy notes you added with your red editor's pen on my pages!

To all you Sistas out there –and there are a lot of you and you know who you are – thank you for your love, prayers, encouragement and your friendships! You are the Sistahood of Jesus Christ! You bless my heart more than I can express. Thank you! I love you all!

In Christ's love and for His glory,

Polly Balint

"Hear, O LORD, and answer me,
for I am poor and needy.
Guard my life,
for I am devoted to you."
Psalm 86:1-2

Table of Contents

The Gospel Stings as it Saves

Grace Balint, one of Polly's daughters, at 3 years old.

"...the gospel of God..."
Romans 1:1

Untouched Bibles are lying around U.S. homes and stores like man-of-wars floating in the ocean. Bibles can be found generously scattered everywhere. Both of these objects produce quite a sting when contact is made with them. Most people realize this and avoid both of them, sometimes at all costs!

The sea creature, man-of-war, looks harmless enough with its small, clear balloon-like body trimmed in pink and blue floating in the salty sea or beached along the shoreline. But it has long, deceptively dangerous tentacles that cause a fiery, long-lasting sting when it touches human skin. There's more bad news: the stringy tentacles leave unsightly, burning welts on the skin. It's wise to find a lifeguard on beach who has an antidote for the painful exposure. There is nothing left to do but wait for the painful sore to heal.

When a person comes in contact with the word of God, there is also a piercing sting; whether the reader knows God or not. Why? Reading the Bible is like looking in the mirror – it is truth and reality. ***"For the word of God is living and active. Sharper than any double-edged sword, it penetrates even to dividing soul and spirit, joints and marrow; it judges the thoughts and attitudes of the heart"*** (Hebrews 4:12). Whew! That's God Power! The power of the gospel message separates the light from the darkness, exposing everything in its wake. We're either going to hate the fact that God knows and sees everything about each one of us or we're going to find great comfort and joy in knowing He loves His children in spite of our wickedness.

Here's the Good News: The gospel offers abundance in our lives, here and now as well as eternally. Copies of the Bible are readily available in the U.S., but people refuse to read them and they use their own rebellion to deny God's existence. The truth is, the Lord knows all, sees all and understands man's ways. "***Am I only a God nearby, declares the LORD, "and not a God far away? Can anyone hide in the secret places so that I cannot see him?" declares the LORD. "Do I not fill heaven and earth?" declares the LORD*** (Jeremiah 23:24).

The gospel was promised in the Old Testament and was fulfilled in the New Testament. God eternally cursed the serpent for deceiving Eve and said, ***"And I will put enmity between you and the woman, and between your offspring and hers; he will crush your head, and you will strike his heel"*** (Genesis 3:15). God promised a victorious crushing blow that would overcome sin through the arrival of His Son Jesus Christ on earth. ***"The gospel he promised beforehand through his prophets in the Holy Scriptures regarding his Son"*** (Romans 1:2-3).

Do we get it yet? ***"God so loved the world that he gave his one and only Son, that whoever believes in him shall not perish but have eternal life"*** (John 3:16). God the Father and His Son Jesus Christ have such a love for each other that they are ***"one"*** (John 17:22). There is a deep love between them. God LOVES His Son. And yet, **"regarding his Son"** (Romans 1:3) –His Precious Son, He let Him suffer a tormenting death, for sinners. God does so love His world and His children.

Jesus is real and He is here. Now. He is HERE. In fact, He is everywhere! Whether we know Him or not. He is everywhere, all the time! ***"Nothing in all creation is hidden from God's sight. Everything is uncovered and laid bare before the eyes of him to whom we must give an account"*** (Hebrews 4:13).

After Jesus rose from the dead He appeared to His disciples and ate fish with them. He spoke to them about the promises of the Old Testament being fulfilled. ***"Then he opened their minds so they could understand the Scriptures. He told them, 'This is what is written: The Christ will suffer and rise from the dead on the third day, and repentance for the forgiveness of sins will be preached in his name to all nations, beginning at Jerusalem***" (Luke 24:45-47).

Wow. God's love for His children is immeasurable. It's so powerful it covers sins. It's unconditional so that we can come to Him just as we are right now. Do you know Him? Do you mock Him? Do you love Him? Are you His?

Sistas, we can't *mess* with God and we surely cannot *mess* with His Son! My Bible says if we do, there's hell to pay and it's going to be a much bigger sting than we could ever get from a man-of-war.

Just Wrath

Tree split by lightning.

"...your wrath against men
brings you praise..."
Psalm 76:10

The LORD is a tenderhearted Shepherd of His people and, at the same time, He is the Almighty God who is the Creator and Controller of the universe. Wow. That's grace and greatness! Those who love and know Him are thankful to call Him LORD. ***"The LORD is compassionate and gracious; slow to anger, abounding in love. He will not always accuse, nor will he harbor his anger forever"*** (Psalm 103:8-9). However, God must not be mocked and tested by our rebellion and disobedience. Frankly, we can't *mess with* God for long because His holiness commands our worship and respect. He commands us to ***"hate evil, for he guards the lives of his faithful ones and delivers them from the hand of the wicked"*** (Psalm 97:10).

God punishes evil. But since He is the God of grace, He warns us. Then He exhorts us again and again giving us more opportunity to flee from sin. He is a *just* God. ***"Turn from evil and do good"*** (Psalm 34:14) He tells us. ***"Woe to those who call evil good and good evil"*** (Isaiah 5:20a), He says. He rises up in judgment and wrath against His enemies. And because God's wrath is *just*, whatever He chooses to do – whether to punish or prosper -- is righteous and good. Think about this: those who have been rescued from their enemies as a result of God's wrath – are going to praise Him! ***"Surely your wrath against men brings you praise"*** (Psalm 76:10a). Who would have thought of celebrating *wrath*? Only a child of God can celebrate the wrath of God. Are you seeing how absolutely amazing He really is? There is no one greater.

There are many examples in Scripture of people who rose up against God with pride and anger and they were faced His wrath. It's called sowing and reaping in Galatians 6:7. In the book of Daniel, King Nebuchadnezzar asked one of his servants, Daniel, to interpret his dream. God had given Daniel great knowledge and wisdom and the ability to ***"understand visions and dreams of all kinds"*** (Daniel 1:17). God used Daniel to warn Nebuchadnezzar he would become like a wild animal and eat grass if he would not

"acknowledge that the Most High is sovereign over the kingdoms of men and gives them to anyone he wishes" (Daniel 4:25b). The Lord – through Daniel – also promised to restore Nebuchadnezzar's kingdom if he would acknowledge God's sovereign power. ***"Renounce your sins by doing what is right, and your wickedness by being kind to the oppressed. It may be that then your prosperity will continue"*** (Daniel 4:27). Instead of humbling himself, one year later King Nebuchadnezzar was ***"walking on the roof of the royal palace of Babylon, he said, 'Is not this the great Babylon I have built as the royal residence, by my mighty power and for the glory of my majesty?'"*** (Daniel 4:29-30). Immediately he was driven away from people and ***"ate grass like cattle...his hair grew like the feathers of an eagle and his nails like the claws of a bird"*** (Daniel 4:33). When God showed him mercy, Nebuchadnezzar's sanity and his kingdom rule were restored. He began to praise God. ***"Now I, Nebuchadnezzar, praise and exalt and glorify the King of heaven, because everything he does is right and all his ways are just. And those who walk in pride he is able to humble***" (Daniel 4:37).

In Scripture God's people pray that He would be faithful to His promises to protect the righteous and destroy the evil coming against them. ***"My shield is God Most High, who saves the upright in heart. God is a righteous judge, a***

God who expresses his wrath every day" (Psalm 7:10-11).

God poured out his wrath with 10 plagues on Pharaoh and the Egyptians because of his hard-heartedness for not letting the Israelites leave their bondage of slavery in Egypt. Then after Pharaoh finally released God's people he changed his mind about letting them go and pursued the Israelites on the dry ground of the parted Red Sea. ***"The water flowed back and covered the chariots and horsemen—the entire army of Pharaoh that had followed the Israelites into the sea. Not one of them survived"*** (Exodus 14:28). After that miracle Moses and the Israelites gave praise to God and sang, ***"I will sing to the LORD, for he is highly exalted. The horse and its rider he has hurled into the sea"*** (Exodus 15:1). Again, His just wrath against men bringing Him praise!

Psalm 76 describes the power of God's sovereign rule over all things. God's people know "***He will judge the world in righteousness; he will govern the peoples with justice"*** (Psalm 9:8). A child of God finds great security knowing Almighty God never stops watching over, protecting and providing for His children's needs.

Whose Agenda Fills Your Calendar?

Starting each day seeking Him.

"Seek first his kingdom..."
Matthew 6:33

Women want to be free. Free of heavy burdens of bondage like: struggling to measure up to the world's ever-changing standards instead of God's expectations, smothering guilt, loneliness, debilitating anxiety and stress. Women want to be free to live fully, love passionately and laugh hilariously. But I believe most women are worn out because we accept lies about ourselves and so we over commit to keep from being judged. We want to please. Most women are *flat worn out* trying to keep up with hectic daily schedules.

On the other hand, let's face it, Sistas, sometimes the reason we're worn out is because we'll always find time to do what WE WANT to do but when it comes time to do something we SHOULD we say we don't have time. No? Hmm. Well, whose agenda has filled up our personal calendar: God's or our own? Do we ever say to ourselves, "Sorry, I'm just too busy!" or "Where did the time go?" or "How am I ever going to get everything done?"

Please note: I am not talking about emergencies that sovereignly and abruptly change our daily schedules. I'm talking about the woman who has taken ownership of the lie that she *has to* live and perform as Super Mom and never allows herself to rest. She's the Woman of Fear who is a reluctant but faithful people-pleaser and will not say "no" even when she is fully aware God has already filled up her calendar with His will for her. Women of all ages fall into this trap.

Why do we stockpile commitments like loads of dirty laundry? Is it just a bad habit that we over commit? Or is our decision making caused by outside influences? Our own thoughts?

Who really is the one who fills in our personal calendars with lunch dates, coffee dates, trips to the mall, long phone conversations, extended music lessons, ball team commitments and practices, neighborhood committee meetings, club membership meetings, addictive hours of those insulting reality shows on cable TV, and even obsessive hours spent on social networking?

Who of us, Sistas, will tune out all of the worldly TV comedy/dramas and tune into God and His word? Do we say "yes" to invitations and commitments when we really don't sense God putting it on our heart to do these things? Do we have people in our lives who pull on us and strongly urge us to come immediately and meet their needs? Are they impatient with their requests? Are they considering your situation at all or do they just demand that you come and do something for them?

Jesus often dealt with anxious people who needed healing. They begged Him to follow them somewhere, to heal them instantly, and they actually pressed into Him in crowds. However the teachings in the Bible clearly show the world that Jesus was totally devoted to His Father's will and not man's agenda. ***"My food is to do the will of him who sent me and to finish his work"*** (John 4:34).

1-Jesus was never in a hurry.

2-Jesus was never ruled or controlled by His circumstances.

3-Jesus was riveted to obeying the voice and instruction of His Heavenly Father, God. His obedience to God gave Him joy,

peace, strength, love, power, supernatural knowledge and wisdom.

4-Jesus' agenda was God's agenda for Him. His social calendar and His personal calendar were filled up by God's will for Him. Because of that Jesus always had peace because He put His life, time, talents, and treasures in God's hands and followed Him. When it was time for Jesus to prepare to join His Father in heaven again, He prayed, ***"I have brought you glory on earth by completing the work you gave me to do"*** (John 17:4).

Whoa. And Jesus, my precious Sistas, is our role model, our example of how to live an abundant life in Christ! We can read in the books of Matthew, Mark, Luke and John about the multitudes that followed the Savior and sort of pulled at Him to do something for them. Does this sound familiar to your own life at times? Me, too! But when I slow down and look to God, He helps me calm down, pray and ask Him to give me wisdom in my decisions. ***"Be still and know I am God"*** (Psalm 46:10). Being still is the only way to clean out our cluttered calendars and get rid of distractions and time-stealing habits.

Do we only 'pencil in' a daily personal devotional time with our LORD so that if something else – like a personal desire – comes up we'll postpone our study and prayer time? Oops. ***"But seek first his kingdom and his righteousness and all these things will be given to you as well"*** (Matthew 6:33). He does meet our needs when we are spiritually drawing from our heavenly Source of Supply.

We can pray and ask Him what we are supposed to do with our time. Then prayerfully wait for the answer. That's the only way we can hear Him -- to be still and listen with our hearts for His voice. That is how we can be free to live the life God has planned for each one of us. Then the blessings of peace, joy and love begin to flow.

A beautiful portrayal of this is found in Luke 10:38-42. It's a familiar, brief passage, and in my opinion it's piercing truth about women's tendencies. Martha invited Jesus to come to her home. As most hostesses tend to do, Martha was scurrying about and was ***"distracted by all the preparations that had to be made"*** (Luke 10:40). Distracted? Yes. Hmm. She also seemed to be angry that her sister Mary who ***"sat at the Lord's feet listening to what he said"*** (Luke 10:39) was not frantically helping her in the preparations. Instead, because Mary was resting herself at the feet of Jesus, she was very relaxed. Hmm. Mary stopped what she was doing, tuned into the words and presence of Jesus and she was peaceful. Time with her LORD was a priority on her calendar.

And Martha? Dear Martha hastily asked Jesus, ***"Lord, don't you care that my sister has left me to do the work by myself? Tell her to help me!"*** (Luke 10:40).

Jesus, in total submission to His Father in heaven, said, ***"Martha, Martha, you are***

worried and upset about many things but only one thing is needed. Mary has chosen what is better and it will not be taken away from her" (Luke 10:41-42). Wow. That's true riches of joy, love, peace...freedom!

God has put a love in my heart for my Sistas. All of my Sistas everywhere! My heart is filled with gratitude to God for continuing to teach me how to make my personal calendar clutter free. It's a long journey but I'm slowly learning! It's definitely a life-long process and worth it, too! I pray and tell Him I want to be free and live that ***"life, and have it to the full"*** as He promises His children (John 10:10). Yes, I want to bring glory to God by living freely, loving passionately and laughing hilariously in this life and I want that for you, too. I really do. This is why I share what's on my heart—with you. May God be glorified!

Worry Wart

Author and Golfer Polly Balint

"Who of you by worrying can add a single hour to his life?"
Matthew 6:27

Let's talk about being a Worry Wart. It's a perfect name, by the way. It's yucky. To worry is to fret, to have anxiety and fear. And it takes a lot of energy to be a Worry Wart. Is it just me or has constant worry become your deluded comfort zone – kind of like how an alcoholic thinks the next drink will be the one that will bring comfort? These are both sinful habits. You want it to go away but you keep picking it back up after you prayerfully lay it down. Sounds like an addiction to me, and that's idolatry.

Idols do not love us back, you know. Have you thought about that? Worry is an idol because worry cannot help our situation, worry cannot heal anything, worry cannot provide for our needs, worry does not love us back, and worry is not a blessing in our lives. That is a description of an idol. Just fill in the idol blank.

Not too long ago, I got to the point in my life that I got so tired of drowning my sorrows in worry that I asked God for relief. Worrying was wearing me out, robbing my joy and hindering me from the work God was calling me to do. Since I knew the powerful Scripture passages about worry, anxiety and fretting; and that ***"The word of God is living and active. Sharper than any double-edged sword"*** (Hebrews 4:12), I knew I was standing on a very strong foundation. ***"Therefore, I tell you, do not worry about your life, what you will eat or drink; or about your body, what you will wear. Is not life more important than food, and the body more***

important clothes? Look at the birds of the air; they do not sow or reap or store away in barns, and yet your heavenly Father feeds them. Are you not much more valuable than they?" (Matthew 6:25-26). Look at that, He commands us, **"do not worry."** So if we worry, we are sinning. It means we aren't trusting God and we begin to fret.

During my deliverance from this bondage, I was on a prayer walk – after my early morning personal devotional time in our family room. I had had enough of the delusion that I *needed* to be worrying. The devil had me in his lying grip until my prayer walk in the neighborhood, and the verse popped in my head, ***"Who of you by worrying can add a single hour to his life?"*** (Matthew 6:27). Wow. I was familiar with that verse but I saw it in a brand new way! That's when I realized my worrying has been an idol in my life. Remember, idols are worthless. That's pretty much what this verse is saying! An idolater ***"feeds on ashes, a deluded heart misleads him; he cannot save himself, or say, 'Is not this thing in my right hand a lie?'"*** (Isaiah 44:20)

Sistas, if you are struggling and you don't understand why you are in some sort of bondage or captivity, or you have been robbed of your joy, ask the LORD to reveal to you what is going on. Ask Him to deliver you and show you the truth about your situation. Remember, we were created to worship something and our hearts are going to connect to something we think is going to take care of our needs and our lives. We worship idols when we are deluded. ***"Those who cling to worthless idols forfeit the grace that could be theirs"*** (Jonah 2:8). We believe the lie and become captives. ***"All who make idols are nothing, and the things they treasure are worthless"*** (Isaiah 44:9a).

Who can imagine that being a Worry Wart is idolatrous? God heard my cries to Him to reveal the truth about my struggles, I confessed my sin of worrying, believed His word, and He rescued me. Now I know to be continually watchful and prayerful about what He has taught me. He can do that for you, too. He is who He says He is.

She Couldn't Be Insulted or Shaken

Mary Balint, one of Polly's daughters, fearlessly taking a leap of faith!

"...even the dogs eat crumbs that fall from their masters' table."
Matthew 15:27

Are you easily offended? Are you quick to lash out at the slightest comment? Does your posture become rigid as you surround yourself with an invisible, defensive wall? Have you ever thought why some people are that way? Sometimes it happens because we are the center of our own attention! There's another name for it: self-centeredness. We get upset about a situation because we have ourselves as the focus instead of the power and promises of God. Self-centeredness gives life to insecurity and confusion. Focusing and trusting in God puts it to death. It's a gnarly net that can ensnare God's children and we can be caught up in our own delusions.

Sometimes it takes the Lord Himself to step into our situations and remind us to look to Him at all times to find our security and well-being. Remember when Jesus reminded Martha –who was frantically preparing to host a meal in her home–to put her eyes on Him and not her circumstance. That's what her sister Mary was doing—everything in Mary was riveted to Jesus and His words –and was she was unshakable as she sat at Jesus' feet. But He said to her sister, ***"Martha, Martha, you are worried about many things but only one thing is needed. Mary has chosen what is better and it will not be taken away from her"*** (Luke 10:41-42). Martha was shaken and offended!

There was a long period of time during my personal prayer and Bible reading that I was intrigued with passages that said, ***"I have set the LORD always before me. Because he is at my right hand, I will not be shaken"*** (Psalm 16:8). I knew I had the Lord with me, too, but I was easily shaken by things in my life. Looking back I can see I was not really believing and applying the word of God to my heart. Several times I read verses like, ***"He alone is my rock and my salvation; he is my fortress, I will never be shaken"*** (Psalm 62:2). There it is again! David said, ***"I saw the Lord always before me.***

Because he is at my right hand, I will not be shaken" (Acts 2:25). I have learned that being shaken is to not have security and a sound mind – it's the opposite of having your confidence in the Lord. ***"Surely he will never be shaken; a righteous man will be remembered forever"*** (Psalm 112:6). Since self-control is one of the fruits of the Spirit, we need to get a grip on our thoughts and emotions and tell our souls to honor God in everything we do. We have to set our minds on our goal and not waiver.

In Matthew 15, a Canaanite woman came to him crying out, ***"Lord, Son of David, have mercy on me! My daughter is suffering terribly from demon-possession"*** (Mark 15:22). Even this pagan woman knew of the Lordship of Jesus Christ. She knew of His power and glory and called on Him to send forth His sovereign power! The disciples were frustrated with her lost soul and Jesus said to them – knowing the woman was not one of His followers – ***"I was sent only to the lost sheep of Israel"*** (Matthew 15:24). Instead of getting her feelings hurt by His comment she called on His holy name again for help, ***"Lord, help me!"*** (Matthew 15:25) She was passionate about this God-Man delivering her afflicted daughter. She continued to seek the Greatest Source of Help and Healing. But after she cried out to Jesus again He said to her, ***"It is not right to take the children's bread and toss it to their dogs"*** (Matthew 15:26).

Jesus called her a dog. Yes. A dog. The Apostle Paul described people who aggressively and destructively opposed the Gospel, dogs. ***"Watch out for those dogs, those men who do evil..."*** (Philippians 3:2). And after Jesus called this Canaanite woman a dog did she run away and cry? No. Did she hide in shame because she was called a dog? No. She was on a mission and she was not going to let anything keep her from her goal. She knew she was not a dog. She knew who she was and she stood on firm ground. She was a mother desperate to see her daughter healed and she went to The Great Physician to heal her. Name calling could not stop her. Hindrances could not stop her. What the crowds were doing and saying about her did not affect her. She could not be shaken. Sistas, are you listening? "***Fear of man***" (Proverbs 29:25) was not in this woman's vocabulary. She responded to Jesus in humility, "***Yes, Lord, but even the dogs eat the crumbs that fall from their masters' table"*** (Matthew 15:27). Her security and well-being were intact as she focused on the Lord as Master. Jesus was pleased with her response to Him. And He told her that her daughter was healed that day because of her great faith. Are you, too, standing on a firm foundation of faith in Jesus Christ so you can't be insulted or shaken?

Pagans Are Blind Drivers

Lexie, Polly's personal assistant

"... so the blind will see and those who see will become blind."
John 9:39

Driving in the dark without headlights is more than dangerous. It's lethal. It's like driving blind; there is no warning of obstacles, roadway signs are unseen, and oncoming traffic can instantly become a five-car pileup. How does anyone even stay in the correct lane? This is what pagans are like, adamantly insisting they don't need a seatbelt during their spiritually blind drive through life. It is a fact that seatbelts save lives and so does Jesus Christ. But pagans don't want the radiance of Christ's presence to light their way. ***"This is the***

verdict: Light has come into the world, but men loved darkness instead of light because their deeds were evil. Everyone who does evil hates the light, and will not come into the light for fear that his deeds will be exposed" (John 3:19-20).

This sounds reckless and hopeless, doesn't it? Life without Christ ***is*** reckless and hopeless. It is spiritual blindness. ***"Jesus said, 'For judgment I have come into this world, so that the blind will see and those who see will become blind"*** (John 9:39). The NIV commentary states that since the presence and life of Jesus "divides people it is a sort of judgment – and those who reject Him end up spiritually blind."

Whether we believe it or not, everybody needs the life and light of Jesus at work inside them! We were created by God, for God. When we try to live according to our own personal rules and agendas, it's like driving through life without brakes. We break all the rules, disrespect authority and we don't stop at warning signs because there is no self control. Self control is a fruit of the Spirit (Galatians 5:23). ***"By their fruit you will recognize them...every good tree bears good fruit, but a bad tree bears bad fruit"*** (Matthew 7:16-17). Only God's people bear the Holy Spirit's fruit.

Our country is recklessly driving down the road to Babylon. We used to be carpooling and faithfully driving the speed limit; obeying all the laws on the King's highway that leads to LIFE. Life was simpler and people were much more content with simple things. However, we have turned off the highway. Now our lifestyles are revved up with worldly obsessions that have us barreling toward a self-centered, power-hungry, materialistic destination. We have made a wrong turn toward Babylon because we are driving in the dark without our lights on. Jesus is the light; and we, as a nation, don't think we need Him anymore. So, here we are in the dark with our law-breaking speed accelerating toward the town of Captivity, also known as Babylon.

Are you and your family praying and preparing for when we get there? For God's people there is always hope. ***"If my people, who are called by my name will humble themselves and pray and seek my face and turn from their wicked ways, then will I hear from heaven and will forgive their sin and will heal their land"*** (2 Chronicles 7:14). All is not hopeless; we are just on a hazardous pilgrimage.

As we journey on our highway to heaven and see blind drivers going the wrong way, we should think, *carpool*! Yes, let's each give those blind drivers a ride to show them what it means to journey through life with our lights on! It's our duty to let them know that God will open their eyes and enlighten them if they repent of their sins and make a U-turn to go the right way! We can tell them what God can do for them: ***"...my God turns my darkness into light"*** (Psalm 18:28). Jesus commands us in the long, glorious message of His ***Sermon on the Mount*** (Matthew 5:1 – Matthew

7:29) to ***"Let your light shine before men that they may see your good deeds and praise your Father in heaven"*** (Matthew 5:16). And although Jesus *is* the light of the entire world, he turns to us to tell His people, ***"You are the light of the world"*** (Matthew 5:14a) so we will carry on His work!

"But whoever lives by the truth comes into the light, so that it may be seen plainly that what he has done has been done through God" (John 3:21). It's only ***"in your light we see light"*** (Psalm 36:9) so let's tighten our seatbelts and drive on reflecting His light!

Preach it, Sista!

Julie Brown, Polly's sister,
speaks at women's conference.

"Go into all the world and
preach the good news..."
Mark 16:15

After God changes our hearts and saves us, He commissions us. He tells us to go tell the ***Good News*** of His birth, life, death, resurrection and His royal return to His heavenly throne. We are to tell the world about the only Savior who literally saves souls and lives in accordance to His sovereign power. We are to go and tell others that Jesus was born in purity and holiness. ***"Joseph son of David, do not be afraid to take Mary home as your wife, because what is conceived in her is from the Holy Spirit. She will give birth to a son, and you are to give him the name Jesus, because he will save his people from their sins"*** (Matthew 1:20-21). He was brutally tortured to show the world the vast wickedness of our sins. ***"The Son of Man must be delivered into the hands of sinful men, be crucified and on the third day be raised again"*** (Luke 24:7). We are to share that God brought His Son back to life and into His heavenly seat of honor at His right hand. Jesus endured all of this torture out of obedience, ***"Father, if you are willing, take this cup from me; yet not my will but yours be done"*** (Luke 22:42).

He is the LORD of life who ***"redeems your life from the pit and crowns you with love and compassion"*** (Psalm 103:4). He is a magnificent protector and full of glorious power. ***"The angel of the LORD encamps around those who fear him, and he delivers them"*** (Psalm 34:7). All of this really is Good News because Jesus offers His hearers abundant life in this life and the next! ***"I have come that they may have life and have it to the full"*** (John 10:10).

Not one Christian is exempt from this commission of sharing the Good News. But it is an assignment that is a privilege and an honor because we are called to tell others ***Good News.*** Why would anyone hesitate to tell someone else good news? It's a simple task. Everyone, I think, would love to hear GOOD news. Right? Hey, I have been in the writing media for decades and news that sells best is news that's not-so-good. Don't believe me? Question: What are the cover stories of the magazines and newspapers in your grocery store checkout lines? Answer: People's personal tragedies, whether they're true or not. Right? In addition, quite often it's hopeless, violent, dramatic or exaggerated accounts of news in the world.

However, my Bible says, **"Go into all the world and preach the good news [gospel] to all creation"** (Mark 16:15). Christians are commanded by God to tell everyone that there is hope, help and healing for their souls, their lives, their families and friends! It's an amazing assignment. It's one He equips us to handle and He teaches us to handle it with grace. His grace, that is. So why is it so hard to throw a drowning soul a life preserver and tell them they don't have to drown in their own despair? Why don't we enthusiastically tell others the truth who have been blinded by worldly lies? What is our fear? Selfishness? We are not going to tell them bad news when we share the gospel, we will tell them good news!

And just think, we don't even have to try to find someone who needs to hear The Good News. These people are right in front of us: in restaurants, shopping malls, grocery stores, dry cleaners, at the drive-thru restaurants, in parks, along jogging paths, in the stands at the ballgames, in our neighborhoods and even in our own families! Yikes! All around us there are hurting, lost, lonely, desperate people who need someone to rescue them from their dark pit of despair. Jesus is the only Savior who can meet their every need with His life, His punishment and death on the cross to take the place of our sins, His resurrection! He can transform their lives when they surrender to Him! ***"This is what is written: The Christ will suffer and rise from the dead on the third day, and repentance and forgiveness of sins will be preached in his name to all nations"*** (Luke 24:46-47). Our own nation needs to be Christianized! We've been called, my Sistas & Brothers, to tell others the Good News. Our prayers and our testimonies to the lost and dying world can tear down the enemy's strongholds. Jesus did not say, "Stop!" Jesus said, "Go!"

Life is Fragile. God is Not.

God's tiny creature made this fragile, intricate web.

"...like a fleeting shadow...
Job 14:2

I believe God speaks to us all the time. He speaks through the magnificence of creation. He speaks to us when we read the Bible. He speaks through melodies of music, through our conversations, through a glance from a stranger, an intricate spider web, an eye-catching billboard and even through our thoughts. But do we hear Him?

And personally, He is speaking to me now as I am hearing more and more details—at the time of this writing—about the horrific shooting spree during a midnight showing in a Colorado, USA, movie theater! One young man broke into the dark theater, set off gas canisters and opened fire on the moviegoers. The news reported 12 people dead, dozens injured and 11 were in critical condition. The ages of the victims ranged from a 6-year old girl to a 51-year-old woman. It was shocking. It was an unthinkable act, but it happened.

Life really is fragile—for all of us. God is not. He is Almighty and we need Him. ***"Man born of woman is of few days and full of trouble. He springs up like a flower and withers away; like a fleeting shadow he does not endure"*** (Job 14:1-2). I think God is reminding us with this tragic news—at least those who are willing to listen to Him—that He is God and we are not. We think we are invincible and sometimes might make thoughtless decisions and lustful choices. We are not invincible. We are very fragile. We have a Creator called God and we are His creatures. We were created by Him and exist for His purposes. He made us out of His love and wisdom. Since we are all sinners living in a sinful world He provided a Savior for His children to be washed clean by the blood of the Savior, Jesus. Then He gave us rules and boundaries to keep us safe and whole, and tells us to live lives that honor Him as our Creator. **"So be careful to do what the LORD your God has commanded you; do not turn aside to the right or to the left. Walk in all the way that the LORD your God has commanded you, so that you may live and prosper and prolong your days in the land that you will**

possess" (Deuteronomy 5:32-33). He truly cares about His children and he ***"delights in the well-being of his servant"*** (Psalm 35:27).

When we *forget* God and listen to the worldly ways of living, we are no longer ***alert*** as God commands us. ***"The sorrows of those increase who run after other gods"*** (Psalm 16:4a). God warns us that life is hard and to be careful to follow His lead. ***"We do not belong to the night or to the darkness. So then, ...let us be alert and self-controlled"*** (1 Thessalonians 5:5-6).

He is constantly warning us because He is gracious and merciful. He even gives us spiritual armor to protect us—but of course we have put it on! After the detailed description in Ephesians of God's protective armor for us, the passage closes this way: ***"With this in mind, be alert and always keep on praying for all the saints"*** (Ephesians 6:18). We must remain alert. Daily. Why? Well, here's another warning from God that makes me shake in my boots: ***"So, if you think you are standing firm, be careful that you don't fall!"*** (1 Corinthians 10:12). We must remind each other to be alert and pray for each other.

We are the body of Christ. We were not created to live as hermits. We are to build each other up. He knows we're weak and frail: one critical word can hurt our feelings; we have streaks of jealousy and fits of temper; we gossip; we lose heart; we get sick; we overindulge; we are easily tempted; we get tired. We are fragile, Sistas! God invites us to ***"cast your***

cares on the LORD and he will sustain you" (Psalm 55:22).

What are we doing with our fragile lives? Are we living them out with the power of God working in us? Are we living lives that are richly filled with His presence? Are we leaving a godly legacy behind us? Or are we wasting our ***"fleeting"*** lives? It's not too late to change. ***"The LORD redeems his servants; no one will be condemned who takes refuge in him"*** (Psalm 34:22). God is able to keep us going. ***"Even to your old age and gray hairs I am he, I am he who will sustain you. I have made you and I will carry you; I will sustain you and I will rescue you"*** (Isaiah 46:4). I have seen this in my own life. The Lord has sustained me countless times through my own personal, hurtful, scary storms and trials. And I'm still here and can see how He helped me! Now I love to share this with sistas in our gatherings and remind them that He has done this for them, too. Wow! It seems He is letting us know we need to get up and get going... for His glory!

"The Son is the radiance of God's glory and the exact representation of his being, sustaining all things by his powerful word" (Hebrews 1:3). Yes, life is fragile but our God is not.

Riveted

Julie Brown, Master Potter, using her gifts
to make HIS name famous.

"... your name and renown are the desires of our hearts."
Isaiah 26:8b

Why would anyone want to be passionate about spending their life making God's name well-known? No one would do that unless they were a faithful child of God. His faithful followers adore Him –no, they absolutely delight in Him – because they know Him. And when His people delight in Him, he is exalted and pleased. ***"Delight yourself in the LORD and he will give you the desires of your heart"*** (Psalm 37:4).

To know the triune God – God the Father, God the Son and God the Holy Spirit –is to love Him! When our relationship with Him deepens we will be more and more willing to sacrifice our self-centeredness so we will live in accordance to His will for each one of us. Wait a minute, that's a lot of self-denial! What if we want to be famous and receive attention and accolades? Well, if that's the case, maybe we're not acknowledging Almighty God's greatness and goodness. ***"He set the earth on its foundations; it can never be moved"*** (Psalm 104:5). He is unstoppable in His love and power. ***"Fire goes before him and consumes his foes on every side. His lightning lights up the world; the earth sees and trembles"*** (Psalm 97:3-4). He literally saves His people from their sins by taking their iniquities onto Himself in a tortuous death. "***God made him who had no sin to be sin for us, so that in him we might become the righteousness of God"*** (2 Corinthians 5:21). Wow. ***"He does not treat us as our sins deserve or repay us according to our iniquities. For as high as the heavens are above the earth, so great is his love for those who fear him"*** (Psalm 103:10-11). What else could anyone want than this? This Majestic Creator of the Universe is greater than all things and then chooses to rescue His children from His own wrath! This is why a faithful Christ follower's heart passionately desires to lift of the name of Jesus. We are humbled at His unconditional love and thankful for His forgiveness! Our hearts become riveted to His will, purposes, and presence in our lives! Wow. We know and believe there is no one more powerful or more loving than God! So we wait for Him to speak and act, ***"Yes, Lord, walking in the way of your laws, we wait for you; your name and renown are the desire of our hearts"*** (Isaiah 26:8). We adoringly wait for Him to—again and again—show His power and love, and then He is glorified with our passionate love for Him. We cry out to Him, "***My soul yearns for you in the night; in the morning my spirit longs for you***" (Isaiah 26:9a).

He is fully aware of our weaknesses and yet, He pours out His love on His children. ***"Lord, you establish peace for us; all that we have accomplished you have done for us"*** (Isaiah 26:12). When our hearts and minds are riveted heavenward, the glittery idols of this world are seen for what they really are; fool's gold. Then a Holy God becomes the passion of our hearts and we are satisfied--in this life and in the next. ***"O LORD, our God, other lords besides you have ruled over us, but your name alone do we honor"*** (Isaiah 26:13).

Have you ever prayed this kind of prayer? "Lord, please use my life and my talents to make your name famous."

Join the Party!

Totally Devoted Sistas celebrating God's blessings on our weekly gatherings.

"...the cheerful heart has a continual feast."
Proverbs 15:15b

It glorifies God when His people are thankful and joyful towards Him. ***"Be joyful always; pray continually; give thanks in all circumstances, for this is God's will for you in Christ Jesus"*** (1 Thessalonians 5:16-18). The LORD deeply loves His people and He wants us delighted in Him! ***"As the Father has loved me, so have I loved you. Now remain in my love. I have told you this so that my joy may be in you and that your joy may be complete"*** (John 15:9, 11).

God loves to see us celebrate Him. It's worship! So why don't we have gatherings with lots of people and lots of food, to just simply celebrate His goodness? It is written in Scripture that "***...the cheerful heart has a continual feast"*** (Proverbs 15:15b). According to the NIV commentary, when we have a cheerful heart, *Life is as joyful and satisfying as the days of a festival.* It's the attitude of our heart that's described here and the fruit is a festival-like life!

In Scripture, a festival was considered a celebration with people and food. God told the Israelites, ***"Three times a year you are to celebrate a festival to me"*** (Exodus 23:14). They were so thankful for God's goodness they had parties! The first festival was the Feast of the Unleavened Bread, commemorating the mass exodus out of their bondage in Egypt. Then God commanded, "***Celebrate the Feast of the Harvest with the firstfruits of the crops you sow in your field"*** (Exodus 23:16a). This was also called the Feast of Weeks because it was held seven weeks after the first festival. They were to celebrate the blessings of the first harvest in the promised land. The third festival, ***"Celebrate the Feast of Ingathering"*** (Exodus 23:16b). This was also called the Feast of Tabernacles or Booths. Since they lived in temporary shelters when God brought them out of Egypt, they celebrated that they had new homes and rejoiced in the produce of the land where He brought them. They gave God glory in their festivals for His generous provision.

What about us today? Do we have any reason to be cheerful today and maybe even organize an informal type of festival to the LORD? ***"A happy heart makes the face cheerful"*** (Proverbs 15:13a). This can be contagious! ***"A cheerful heart is good medicine"*** (Proverbs 17:22a). There are even confirmed physical benefits from having a thankful attitude. Good health! ***"A cheerful look brings joy to the heart, and good news gives health to the bones"*** (Proverbs 15:30). Could you imagine what a festive gathering would be like with everyone having a cheerful heart toward God? It would be an amazing party! God wants us to celebrate His love for us. He celebrates us – in His own way – He ***"delights in the well-being of his servants"*** (Psalm 35:27). Remember the Israelites endured so many suffering trials as we all do, but God never lets us go, He carries us when we need His strength to persevere. When Ezra read the Book of the Law of Moses to the Israelites, they wept in remorse for their past sins. "***Nehemiah said, 'Go and enjoy choice food and sweet drinks, and send some to those who have nothing prepared. This day is sacred to our Lord. Do not grieve for the joy of the LORD is your strength'"*** (Nehemiah 8:10). So it is for us today. Our thankfulness and joy in God gives us strength, energy and encouragement. We should celebrate it. My mother had a cheerful heart and she could make anything a festival. If we stopped for ice cream and sat under an umbrella together to devour the creamy treats, she'd say, "Look, we're having a party!" Or if we were gathered around a swimming pool eating hamburgers she'd say the same thing! Her life was a continual feast and she wanted my four siblings and me to learn that if we had a cheerful heart we could have our lives be as joyful and satisfying as the days of a festival. What about you? Do you want that for your family? Then look to God and look at His greatness and His goodness in how He provides for you and protects you and loves you as His child. If you don't know Him as LORD you can join in a festive life with Jesus if you repent of your sins and call on the name of Jesus to forgive you and He will supernaturally adopt you as His child, too. Join the party. It never stops. There is always something to be joyful and thankful for when you are His.

Are You A Good Waiter?

Staff of waiters

"I waited patiently for the LORD"
Psalm 40:1

Someone who is willing to wait for God's answer to a prayer is a person who trusts God. This person doesn't get anxious but instead faithfully perseveres in prayer and hope. ***"I waited patiently for the LORD; he turned to me and heard my cry"*** (Psalm 40:1). God always answers the prayers of His people. That's why He tells us to wait because He plans to answer us in accordance with His will. We must believe He is the Creator and Controller of the entire universe and that He knows exactly what He is doing all the time. It's called His sovereign plan. He's working it out in all of our lives. That's why He tells us to wait. Wait because ***"we know that in all things God works for the good of those who love him, who have been called according to his purpose"*** (Romans 8:28).

But most people hate to wait! And God speaks to us: ***"Be still before the LORD and wait patiently for him"*** (Psalm 37:7a). We are living in an instant gratification society. We don't want to wait in line in a drive-through restaurant, a bank, the dry cleaners, or any other kind of waiting! Singles do not like to wait long for Mr. or Mrs. Right; they want to get married now to Mr. or Mrs. Has Potential. They're not remembering God is sovereign and He may be setting up their perfect mate and He has planned for them to meet at the perfect time!

We don't like to wait for long stop lights, not realizing that God may be detaining us at that long stop light because He is protecting us from imminent danger further down the road. Almighty God really is in control of all things. Jesus told the disciples, ***"All authority in heaven and on earth has been given to me"*** (Matthew 28:18). There is no higher authority than this, and this is where we should be putting our hope. It's His world and His timing for all things.

We don't like to have to wait for tables at restaurants, either. Recently my husband Don and I were on a wonderful date in a cozy, local restaurant that had charming atmosphere. As we started to eat our appetizers there were only a few empty tables. By the time we were eating our tasty entrees there were people crowding the front door and even leaning against the wall next to the hostess station. Others were sitting outside on benches waiting for their names to be called to come in and dine. These guests at the hostess station were frowning. Frowning! I thought to myself, "What's wrong with them? Don't we go out for a nice dinner to have a good time and relax and enjoy good food that we didn't have to cook?" These disgruntled couples were staring at the rest of us as we were enjoying delicious food and drink! They were frowning because they did not want to wait for a table. They wanted a table *now*. There was no danger of the restaurant running out of food. The weather was beautiful outside so they weren't soaking wet from intense humidity or a downpour of rain. They looked to be healthy and they were out with their friends. But they were complaining because they had to wait for a table! It made me laugh to see their scrunched up faces when I realized why they were upset.

I think we can easily wear ourselves out physically and mentally from our own angry impatience! We fret and worry about our lives. We fret and worry about the lives of our family members and our friends. It can be exhausting to try to control situations that surround us! But God tells us, ***"...those who hope in the LORD will renew their strength. They will soar on wings like eagles; they will run and not grow weary, they will walk and not be faint***" (Isaiah 40:31). To wait is to hope.

"I wait for the LORD, my soul waits, and in his word I put my hope. My soul waits for the LORD more than watchmen wait for the morning, more than watchmen wait for the morning" (Psalm 130:5-6). He is worth the wait.

Reflecting His Radiance

Grace Balint, one of Polly's daughters,
radiates His light with her musical talents!

"...I am the light of the world."
John 8:12

Jesus told His disciples to join Him in His Father's work on earth. ***"As long as it is day, we must do the work of him who sent me. Night is coming, when no one can work. While I am in the world, I am the light of the world"*** (John 9:4). His disciples – and all of His followers who were to come—were also instructed to carry on the work after he returned to His heavenly throne. He said, "***You are the light of the world"*** (Matthew 5:14). With His light and presence radiating in His followers, He tells us to ***"Let your***

light shine before men, that they may see your good deeds and praise your Father in heaven" (Matthew 5:16).

Jesus is a deliverer. ***"I have come into the world as a light, so that no one who believes in me should stay in darkness"*** (John 12:46). He removes our darkness and fills His children with ***"the light of life"*** (John 8:12). Sistas, to be walking in His light is to have joy and vitality. He gives us the privilege to live fully. For a child of God to say, ***"The Lord is my light"*** (Psalm 27:1) is to declare deliverance from death, darkness, shame and misery. According to the NIV Study Bible Commentary on Psalm 27:1, the word *light often symbolizes well-being or life and salvation. To say, 'The Lord is my light" is to confess confidence in Him as the source of these benefits.*

Jesus gives His children that supernatural radiance so we will be compelled to ***"Do everything without complaining or arguing, so that you may become blameless and pure, children of God without fault in a crooked and depraved generation, in which you shine like stars in the universe..."*** (Philippians 2:14-15). We are to reflect His light! ***"Whoever follows me will never walk in darkness, but will have the light of life"*** (John 8:12). Imagine! We are carrying the radiant power of God in us, the same power that raised Jesus from the dead!

Consider walking into a room of joy-filled Christians attending an event. As more faithful followers of Christ gather, the "light" gets brighter, spiritually speaking, because the atmosphere of the room grows more and more peaceful and joyful. Then a guest enters whose spiritual life is dark, and you can guess that guest probably won't stay too long. Why? ***"Everyone who does evil hates the light, and will not come into the light for fear that his deeds will be exposed.*** (John 3:20). This is the main reason Christians are rejected in conversations with unbelievers.

This is why unbelievers won't attend church. Darkness hates the light. That's why even faithful Christians experience sorrows and struggles in addition to abundant joys and blessings. We live in a spiritually dark world. It seethes and hisses at the thought of bowing to a Righteous King named Jesus Christ! When was the last time you witnessed to a non-believer? How did they respond? "***But whoever lives by the truth comes into the light, so that it may be seen plainly that what he has done has been done through God"*** (John 3:21).

We must not stop shining the light of hope to a lost and dying world! ***"Those who are wise will shine like the brightness of the heavens, and those who lead many to righteousness, like the stars for ever and ever"*** (Daniel 12:3). It's not our job to save people. He calls us to shine His light and tell others about Him. It's Jesus who saves and He will be with us with our every step.

"Then the righteous will shine like the sun in the kingdom of their Father" (Matthew 13:43). Because He lives in us we will never stop shining!

What's So Bad about Gossip?

Two of Polly's sweet and adorable grandnieces.

"When words are many, sin is not absent..."
Proverbs 10:19

Have you ever had someone tell you personal information about another person and then tell you the reason they shared it with you was so you could pray? Frankly, if I want someone to know something personal about me, I tell them myself. Or if I want to share personal information with a group of trusted friends, I'll ask the group to pray because ***"a trustworthy man keeps a secret"*** (Proverbs 11:13b). I believe anything else is gossip. ***"Gossip betrays a confidence so avoid a man who talks too much"*** (Proverbs 20:19).

Here's another thing I learned: if an acquaintance is constantly telling you entrusted information about another friend, you can be sure they are gossiping about you, too. ***"When words are many, sin is not absent"*** (Proverbs 10:19b). Why do we do it? It's our own pride and insecurity. If we criticize our neighbor we think it makes us look better. We also believe we are steering the focus onto someone else's situation so we don't have to deal with our sinful habits. So now the sin has doubled: we have gossiped and we are prideful. ***"Before his downfall a man's heart is proud"*** (Proverbs 18:12a). And if we are exaggerating while we are gossiping, then we are lying, too! ***"A lying tongue hates those it hurts, and a flattering mouth works ruin"*** (Proverbs 26:28). Whew, this sin stuff is contagious and destructive! It is also wicked and often creates crushing pain for the sinner and the one who is being sinned against. I think we can all relate. This is nasty stuff. Talk about hurt feelings and ruined reputations! What about broken relationships? ***"A gossip separates close friends"*** (Proverbs 16:28b).

Our God hates sin. He showed the world just how heinous it is through the violent death of His precious Son. It took a perfect Savior to be vigorously tortured on a cross to do away with the sins of His people. Yes, sin is ugly. God constantly warns us to avoid evil. ***"Keep your tongue from evil and your lips from speaking lies"*** (Psalm 34:13).

When someone is sharing gossip with us we have a choice to join in the verbal lynching or to refuse to listen. ***"Without wood a fire goes out; without gossip a quarrel dies down"*** (Proverbs 26:20). What do we do when we discover someone is spreading gossip about us? God has an answer for that, too! ***"For it is God's will that by doing good you should silence the ignorant talk of foolish men"*** (1 Peter 2:15). Wisdom says let God take care of it. We need to continue to show ***"soundness of speech that cannot be condemned, so that those who oppose you may be ashamed because they have nothing bad to say about us"*** (Titus 2:8).

As God's children, we should be doing everything we can to build up the body of Christ, not tear it down! We are in a universal, spiritual war and it's the light versus the darkness! ***"Love must be sincere. Hate what is evil; cling to what is good. Be devoted to one another in brotherly love. Honor one another above yourselves"*** (Romans 12:9-10). Our hearts and lives must be focused on the Lord Jesus Christ and His purposes. He will deal with the gossipmongers. ***"Live such good lives among the pagans that, though they accuse you of doing wrong, they may see your good deeds and glorify God on the day he visits us"*** (1 Peter 2:12). God's way is always the best way.

Does Your Heart Sing at Work?

Michelle Evans, co-owner of Salon 20 in Canton, GA, always sings while she works!

"Sing joyfully to the LORD, you righteous;"
Psalm 33:1

There's a sidewalk that lines a portion of the golf course in our neighborhood. Often it is well-traveled by joggers, walkers, and dog owners. Anyone using the narrow concrete path is privileged to enjoy the beauty of the trees, flowering bushes and rolling green fairways. One day during my early morning walk/jog along the sidewalk I heard loud singing coming from the golf course. I looked over to one of the landscaped slopes and there was a maintenance employee singing loudly over the roar of his small truck. He was moving the tee markers out of the way so he could mow the tee box. He was joyfully singing in Spanish. As I continued to walk past him I thought: 'his song was a song of joy!' He was focused on his work and he was singing! It was such a delight because to me, it was rare. How many people sing while they are working? I know employees in corporate offices would get in trouble for singing aloud! But think about this: do our *hearts* sing while we are working? Or are we grumbling and complaining because we are at work? ***"Sing and make music in your heart to the Lord, always giving thanks to God the Father for everything, in the name of our Lord Jesus Christ"*** (Ephesians 5:19b-20).

I slowed down my pace to continue listening to him. I was really enjoying pondering this experience. I thought, 'how refreshing this is to hear someone singing out loud! He doesn't care who is watching or who is listening. He wants to sing!' Who does that? Not many people these days, I don't think.

I also thought about how this man seemed to be grateful to have a job and thankful to be able to work! It made me think of the entitlement attitudes of our culture. We think we deserve –and often demand–instant gratification of our every desire.

And when we don't get immediate results we grumble. But this middle-aged man was contented. It really was a beautiful experience for me. I was so thankful to have been there at that moment because it energized and encouraged me to keep a song in my heart, too!

It brings God glory when we have His song in our hearts, ***"Sing joyfully to the Lord, you righteous; it is fitting for the upright to praise him"*** (Psalm 33:1). Our hearts will sing when our focus is on Him. ***"Shout for joy to the Lord, all the earth. Worship the Lord with gladness; come before him with joyful songs"*** (Psalm 100:1-2).

I don't know if that maintenance man knows the Lord as his Savior but I do know he was used by God to remind me that it pleases Him when we are free to share our joy without the thought of what others might think. ***"He put a new song in my mouth, a hymn of praise to our God. Many will see and fear and put their trust in the Lord"*** (Psalm 40:3).

Trading Our Treasures

Sweet Sista Diane Oberkrom, Founder of
The Soul Food Market in Canton, GA.

"... who does not give up everything he has cannot be my disciple..."
Luke 14:33

We must count the cost of our salvation. The question is: Are we willing to pay the price to become a faithful Christ-follower? Will we love God more than anything or anyone else? ***"Love the Lord your God with all your heart and with all your soul and with all your mind. This is the first and greatest commandment"*** (Matthew 22:37-38).

Our payment is to give up our worldly treasures of self-centeredness, personal agendas, idols of materialism, and sinful lifestyles. ***"Therefore, if anyone is in Christ, he is a new creation; the old has gone, the new has come!"*** (2 Corinthians 5:17). We are changed! He takes us from worldliness to godliness. "***Do not conform any longer to the pattern of this world, but be transformed by the renewing of your mind"*** (Romans 12:2). We will begin to think, act and live differently. The LORD becomes our treasure. ***"So from now on we regard no one from a worldly point of view"*** (2 Corinthians 5:16).

Every Christ-follower is blessed with privileges of knowing God personally and of inheriting God's promises. So basically, there is no limit to what God can do and will do, for His glory and for our good! Only God's people have the power of the Holy Spirit to help them. In addition, God ***"is able to do immeasurably more than all we ask or imagine, according to his power that is at work within us"*** (Ephesians 3:20). God offers abundant life to His children; to be supremely enriched here on earth and eternally in heaven!

Not only are we to surrender our own selfishness, we must even deny our love for our own family members and friends if our love for them is deeper than our love for God! ***"If anyone comes to me and does not hate his father and mother, his wife and children, his brothers and sisters—yes, even his own life—he cannot be my disciple*"** (Luke 14:26). Ouch! If our hearts are not changed, this is impossible! We are born with hearts of stone and only Jesus can turn them into soft, pliable hearts of flesh that will be willing to change and obey Him. When He changes our hearts we begin a new life in Christ, ***"that those who live should no longer live for themselves but for him who died for them and was raised again"*** (2 Corinthians 5:15).

His Holy Word gives very clear instructions to surrender all to Him because he "***who does not give up everything he has cannot be my disciple"*** (Luke 14:33). It's very difficult for us to give up our wants because ***"all have sinned"*** (Romans 3:23). It happened to a rich young ruler who asked Jesus, ***"'Good teacher, what must I do to inherit eternal life?'"*** (Luke 18:18). Although he told Jesus he kept all of the commandments, Jesus replied, "'***You still lack one thing. Sell everything you have and give to the poor, and you will have treasure in heaven. Then, come follow me'"*** (Luke 18:22). The wealthy man was sad and didn't want to give up his worldly treasures ***"because he was a man of great wealth. Jesus looked at him and said, 'How hard it is for the rich to***

enter the kingdom of God!'" (Luke 18:23-24). Jesus warns, ***"Do not store up for yourselves treasures on earth, where moth and rust destroy and where thieves break in and steal. But store up for yourselves treasures in heaven, where moth and rust do not destroy, and where thieves do not break in and steal. For where your treasure is, there your heart will be also"*** (Matthew 6:19-21).

The Apostle Paul knew Christ intimately as His Lord, Savior, Friend and Treasure. He was passionately grateful to Christ for His saving grace. ***"But whatever was to my profit I now consider loss for the sake of Christ. What is more, I consider everything a loss compared to the surpassing greatness of knowing Christ Jesus my Lord, for whose sake I have lost all things. I consider them rubbish, that I may gain Christ and be found in him..."*** (Philippians 3:7-9a).

When we count the cost of following Christ we may find that if we give up our worldly treasures, the world will hate us, just as it hated Jesus. We may lose some friends, as Jesus did. He told His disciples, ***"If you belonged to the world, it would love you as its own. As it is, you do not belong to the world, but I have chosen you out of the world. That is why the world hates you"*** (John 15:19).

The benefits of trading in our worldly treasures for heavenly ones will be a life overflowing with God's unconditional love, grace, forgiveness, peace, protection, provision and total security. ***"I have chosen you and have not rejected you. So do not fear, for I am with you; do not be dismayed, for I am your God. I will strengthen you and help you; I will uphold you with my righteous right hand"*** (Isaiah 41:9c-10). Have you traded in your treasures for true riches?

Hokey Pokey Life

Polly's mother, Mary Gillette Brown,
a woman who was full of love and life!

"Commit your ways to the LORD..."
Psalm 37:5

Why do we say we will commit to something while at the same time we are thinking that if it gets too hard we'll just walk away? We don't like a commitment that includes both of our feet; let's just have one foot in and the other foot out. And if things get testy then we'll take the other foot out. If the circumstances become calm again we might put one foot back into the so-called commitment. We don't want to put our whole self in! No thank you. What if I don't like that dance anymore?

That is not what Jesus teaches His people. Faithfulness is one of the fruits of the Spirit of God. ***"And without faith it is impossible to please God, because anyone who comes to him must believe that he exists and that he rewards those who earnestly seek him"*** (Hebrews 11:6). When we commit ourselves to Christ we receive immeasurable promises and benefits of being His. He tells us to ***"Commit your way to the LORD; trust in him and he will do this: He will make your righteousness shine like the dawn and the justice of your cause like the noonday sun"*** (Psalm 37:5). He wants us all *in*! He wants to give us a radiant life!

We must commit ourselves to God in every way. King Asa was told, ***"Because you relied on the king of Aram and not on the LORD your God, the army of the king of Aram has escaped from your hand. Were not the Cushites and Libyans a mighty army with great numbers of chariots and horsemen?***

Yet when you relied on the LORD, he delivered them into your hand. For the eyes of the LORD range throughout the earth to strengthen those whose hearts are fully committed to him" (2 Chronicles 16:7b-9a). He wants a full commitment from us as His people!

My mother was committed to loving and caring for me and my four siblings after my dad walked out the door. I was very young when that happened. He never came back home again. But my mother kept us together like a hen gathers her chicks under her wings. We had issues and struggles from the brokenness without a daddy in our home but Mom insisted on keeping us together; daily cooking huge meals for us, caring for us in every way she knew, and even seasonally taking all of us on beach vacations and to refreshingly cool mountain cabins. Mom's heart was broken and she was so tired from taking care of her large, lively household by herself, but she kept on loving us and caring for us. And most of that time she was either smiling or laughing. She made a commitment and God was blessing it. God was "***A father to the fatherless, a defender of widows***" (Psalm 68:5). He was overseeing our household.

Mom loved to play golf and was an excellent player. She told me investors came to her and offered to sponsor her on the pro golf tour. She turned them down because she said she would not leave her five children. I remember thinking when she told me that she must really love us a lot!

She dated a couple of men over the years. I remember one man who was a very successful businessman. When we didn't hear about him anymore I asked her about him, and she said he wanted to marry her, leave us with a hired nanny, and have her travel with him all over the world. She said she wouldn't leave her children behind. Her love and commitment to the five of us was more powerful than all her trials and hardships from being deserted by her husband. ***"To the faithful you show yourself faithful***" (Psalm 18:25). God honored Mom's faithful commitment to love and care for her children. He gave her the ability to keep on going. ***"I can do everything through him who gives me strength"*** (Philippians 4:13).

Mom loved all kinds of music. She absolutely loved to sing, and she danced with great rhythm! But I guarantee you her favorite dance was not the Hokey Pokey. She was all *in* and stayed *in* until the end. God made it possible.

The Good Kind of Change

Polly's husband Don, their daughters Mary & Grace (holding Lexie.)

"...I no longer live, but Christ lives in me."
Galatians 2:20

Have you ever seen an active, capable woman and asked yourself, "How is she able to do all of that?" Maybe she's Super Woman. Or maybe she's Wonder Mom! No, she may have the gift of organization or is a good steward of her time, but her abilities still come from God. We really can't take credit for anything we accomplish. Not one thing. We won't believe this unless we are spiritually connected to the Lord, as a branch is attached to a fruitful vine. In fact, Jesus said, ***"'I am the vine; you are the branches. If a man remains in me and I in him, he will bear much fruit; apart from me you can do nothing'"*** (John 15:5). And we become like an overflowing fruit basket when we are His and obey His commands. ***"'If you remain in me and my words remain in you, ask whatever you wish, and it will be given to you. This is to my Father's glory, that you bear much fruit showing yourselves to be my disciples'"*** (John 15:7-8).

We only really discover this when we become a child of God through the confession and forgiveness of our sins and the turning to Jesus Christ as our Lord and Savior. Then we are changed. ***"I have been crucified with Christ and I no longer live, but Christ lives in me. The life I live in the body, I live by faith in the Son of God, who loved me and gave himself for me"*** (Galatians 2:20).

It is worldly thinking to think greatness comes from people. Any greatness in people comes from God. We have been created by God to worship Him – but if we are not a child of God we will usually worship people; perhaps they are highly talented or well-known celebrity types of the world. The world sells and markets materialism to our society. And

Baby, we are buying it and heavily going into debt to keep up with the latest and greatest item on the worldly market. We often buy into the idea that this is what gives value to our lives. Not true. Worldly wealth or ***"treasures on earth, where moth and rust destroy, and where thieves break in and steal"*** (Matthew 6:19) are worthless.

"For you were once darkness, but now you are light in the Lord. Live as children of light (for the fruit of the light consists in all goodness, righteousness and truth) and find out what pleases the Lord" (Ephesians 5:8-10). When we are saved by the blood of Christ we really are changed inside and out. His light shines in us and the radiance speaks in our dark world.

I became a Christian during the last few days of my job as a feature writer for a South Florida newspaper. Immediately I moved to Georgia, met, fell in love with and married an amazing, godly man who blesses my life every day! Two years after marrying we took a family vacation to south Florida, and on the way to see more family members, we stopped by the newspaper offices where I used to work. It was a Saturday but since it was a daily newspaper I knew there would be a few staff members there. I entered the building and went up the newsroom. I didn't know what to expect but I was curious. I took a sweeping tour through the newsroom. On my way out, the columnist whose desk was still positioned at the entrance of the newsroom as it was a few years ago said to me, "It's great to see you, Polly, but you know what? You are not the same person who used to work here." I was dumbfounded and asked him to repeat what he said. He did. I smiled and left. When I reached our car I said to my husband, "What does that mean?" He said it was a compliment. I was really changed by Christ. I had the peace of God, and I was shining His light. It was nothing I did. It's what God did in me. Hallelujah!

Child-like Faith is Mature Faith

Polly's precious grandnieces during a family gathering.

"...whoever humbles himself like this little child..."
Matthew 18:4

Children are a ***"reward"*** from God (Psalm 127:3). They can instantly light up a room with their joy and energy. Their smiles and cheerful chatter can change a grumpy adult into a grateful soul.

Young children represent new life, a new generation who can carry on the promises of God. It was children's praises who ***"silence the foe and the avenger"*** (Psalm 8:2) after Jesus cleared His temple of moneychangers who had turned His ***"house of prayer***" into a ***"den of robbers"*** (Matthew 21:13). The ***"blind and lame came to him at the temple, and he healed them. But when the chief priests and teachers of the law saw the wonderful things he did and the children shouting in the temple area, 'Hosanna to the Son of David,' they were indignant"*** (Matthew 21:14-15). There must have been way too much joy in the house! They grumbled at the joyful noise! Hah! ***"'Do you hear what these children are saying?' They asked him. 'Yes,' Jesus replied, 'have you never read, 'From the lips of children and infants you have ordained praise?'"*** (Matthew 21:16)

This does not mean young, vibrant, beautiful children are innocent. Nope. Not one. ***"Surely I was sinful at birth, sinful from the time my mother conceived me"*** (Psalm 51:5). We are talking about children being delightfully alive and free from their burdens because they love and fully trust God as their Father. Child-like faith in God the Father is like watching young children who are fully aware they are dependent on others to meet their needs; physically, spiritually and emotionally. Young children cannot drive themselves to the grocery store and push the huge shopping cart!

They can't safely cook a meal by themselves while standing on stool and leaning over a hot stove. They can't walk down to the street corner, hop on a bus, go to the mall and buy clothes for school. Small children are not able to fully protect themselves from danger. They need a parent to help them accomplish what they are trying to do. And they know it; young children are willing to *accept help* in meeting their needs. Young children need care, protection, love and all kinds of provisions for their very lives. In humility they have to look to their caretakers to meet these needs. Yes, humility!

This is what Jesus is saying to his disciples when they came to him to ask***: 'Who is the greatest in the kingdom of heaven?' He called a little child and had him stand among them. And he said: 'I tell you the truth, unless you change and become like little children, you will never enter the kingdom of heaven. Therefore, whoever humbles himself like this child is the greatest in the kingdom of heaven'"*** (Matthew 18:1-4). Humility is the key! God wants all of His children – from the very young to the very old – to humble ourselves, and joyfully and gratefully look to Him as our Sovereign Protector and Provider.

Child-like faith is not *immature* faith. Child-like faith is mature faith. It is wise to have this kind of faith. It believes God the Father is in total control of all things. It buds, blossoms and bears fruit in the Father's unconditional love. It's obeying God's instructions. We cannot have child-like faith unless we ***humble*** ourselves. A Christian knows and believes what Jesus teaches: ***"... apart from me you can do nothing."*** (John 15:5c). As a child of God we will always need our Father! He says to be separate from the darkness of unbelievers and He ***"will be a Father to you, and you will be my sons and daughters, says the Lord Almighty"*** (2 Corinthians 6:18). It's just like the fact that God gave my own family two daughters and they will always be our children–members of our family—no matter where they go, what they do, and no matter what their ages! It's the same with God the Father; when anyone is birthed into His kingdom they will always be His and Jesus says, ***"no one can snatch them out of my Father's hand"*** (John 10:29). He will always be our Father!

Have you ever seen a four-year-old girl walking down a busy shopping mall corridor alone with a designer bag on her arm – and her bag is full of cash and credit cards? She's on her own because she insisted she doesn't need her parent's help. Do you think she's safe all alone? Do you think she'll be able to get one item off a clothes rack? Do you think she can see over the checkout counter? Do you think she could be easily tempted to by a stranger who is lying to her? Hmmmm. Not so funny, is it? This is what we sistas look like when we push our Heavenly Father away and insist on going our own way. We don't listen to His voice. We hear the voice of a stranger who wants to lead us into darkness!

On the other hand, humble, dependent, child-like faith is mature faith that will keep us safe because we are listening to our Father's voice. ***"Whoever listens to me will live in safety and be at ease, without fear of harm"*** (Proverbs 1:33). Wow! Who wouldn't want the freedom, vitality and joy of a child that only comes from whole-heartedly trusting her Father in heaven? I know I do!

She's Truth Hungry

Mary Balint, third from left, celebrating life at a wedding reception with three Becker sisters!

"..the truth will set you free"
John 8:32

She has a major case of battle fatigue from believing lies from her dark enemy. She's been absorbing these lifelong lies about herself: that she's worthless, good-for-nothing, and unforgiveable. She is truth hungry! Sometimes it's so hard for her to feed herself the truth of God's word because she's exhausted from trying to resist the deceitful voices screaming in her head. Sometimes she gives into the lies and then clothes herself in guilt, shame, fear and anxiety. Her weariness wakes up her old belief system and it creates sleepless nights. Even her daylight hours seem drag on and on.

However, since she's a Christ-follower, this doesn't happen to her every day, it's just when she doesn't put on the spiritual armor of God (Ephesians 6:10-18) which protects her spiritually from head to toe. That only happens if she puts is on. ***"If you hold onto my teaching, you are really my disciples. Then you will know the truth and the truth will set you free"*** (John 8:31b-32). The blood of her Savior Jesus Christ has washed her clean and He has delivered her from a deep dark abyss. Her relentless enemy – the enemy of all of God's people – lies to her so she'll fall back into her dark pit of despair. He thinks he can rob Jesus of this adorable trophy of His grace. But that's not going to happen. She is a follower of the Good Shepherd Jesus Christ and He says of His sheep, ***"My sheep listen to my voice; I know them and they follow me. I give them eternal life, and they shall never perish; no one can snatch them out of my hand"*** (John 10:27-28). She is no longer a pit dweller; she lives in ***"green pastures"*** and Jesus ***"restores her soul"*** (Psalm 23:2-3).

She has the Holy Spirit living inside of her and He reminds her to put her eyes back on Jesus, the source of all truth. ***"I am the way, and the truth and the life"*** (John 14:6).

She cries out to God in prayer and He always hears her. She begins to feed herself of the truth of Scripture. ***"The righteous cry out, and the***

LORD hears them; he delivers them from all their troubles" (Psalm 34:17). He reminds her of His love and faithfulness. ***"The LORD your God is with you, he is mighty to save. He will take great delight in you, he will quiet you with his love, he will rejoice over you with singing"*** (Zephaniah 3:17). He is her sovereign protector. ***"You, dear children, are from God and have overcome them, because the one who is in you is greater than the one who is in the world"*** (1 John 4:4). He is compassionate. ***"Because of the Lord's great love we are not consumed, for his compassions never fail. They are new every morning; great is your faithfulness"*** (Lamentations 3:22-23). He removes her fears. ***"The LORD is my light and my salvation—whom shall I fear? The LORD is the stronghold of my life—of whom shall I be afraid?"*** (Psalm 27:1) He is good to her. ***"Taste and see that the LORD is good and blessed is the man [sista] who takes refuge in him"*** (Psalm 34:8). He promises to ***"surround [her] me with songs of deliverance" (***Psalm 32:7b). And He does. He turns her ***"mourning into gladness"*** (Jeremiah 31:13b).

She sings. ***"I waited patiently for the LORD; he turned to me and heard my cry. He lifted me out of the slimy pit, out of the mud and mire; he set my feet on a rock and gave me a firm place to stand. He put a new song in my mouth, a hymn of praise to our***

God. Many will see and fear and put their trust in the LORD" (Psalm 40:1-3). The sista has been fed the truth of God's word. Yes, it is the LORD who ***"fills the hungry with good things"*** (Psalm 107:9). Then she is satisfied and He is glorified.

We Have to Do *Something*!

Ingredients to make egg salad.
Have to do something to make it happen!

"Stretch out your hand"
Matthew 12:13

Have you ever heard anyone say, "I know I need to read my Bible daily and spend quiet time with the Lord because I really want to know Him more deeply; but I don't have time!" Uh-oh. I don't think that will stand up in heaven when we're face to face with Jesus.

No, we seem to find time to shop for bargains, meet a friend for coffee, spend time social networking, play our favorite sport, and watch our favorite cable TV program that has lured us into faithful weekly attendance in front of the flat screen! Yes, we seem to make time for what we like to do. Hmmm. We don't seem to have the time for things that require work, faithfulness and perseverance. Maybe it's just me who does that. Yes, I'm sure that I'm the only one who can easily do another load of laundry or unload the dishwasher instead of Bible reading and praying. I'm the only one who would rather get on the phone instead of going to God's throne. Ouch. Stepping on toes?

We whine and complain because we are not getting what we want --- but we are not faithful to do what God teaches us to do: be wise. Do what it takes to get what you want. Do you need to get up and work smarter, pray, exercise, make phone calls, study, plan, budget? We are not doing anything to work toward what we desire. It's like someone sitting on a sofa for hours wildly shaking a remote control at their TV set, saying, "Lord, why don't I have a job? Why aren't you hearing my prayer?" And this person did not compose a resume, or search for a job in the newspapers or online. They say they want a job but they won't do anything to get it. ***"You do not have, because you do not ask God. When you ask, you do not receive because you ask with wrong motives, that you may spend what you get on your pleasures"*** (James 4:2d-3).

Well, it's definitely easier to complain than to stop, pray and call on God for wisdom and guidance. It's easier to complain about our poor health habits than to get up and walk around the block every day.

What about someone who has an addiction? It's time to move away from those who are addicts and find friends who are edifying. There's the student who will not study for a test and then the morning of the test, the student says, "Lord, help me get an A on the test!" There is always something we must do to reach our heart's desire. God gives us promises and He also gives us the ability to get up and do something about it. Need wisdom? ***"For the LORD gives wisdom, and from His mouth come knowledge and understanding. He holds victory in store for the upright, He is a shield to those whose walk is blameless, for He guards the course of the just and protects the way of His faithful ones"*** (Proverbs 2:6-8).

When Jesus was walking into a synagogue, "***a man with a shriveled hand was there"*** (Matthew 12:10). Jesus said to him, ***"'Stretch out your hand.' So he stretched it out and it was completely restored, just as sound as the other"*** (Matthew 12:13). How did the man stretch out a shriveled hand? The man had to *do something* in order to be healed.

When we are saved from eternal damnation because we have sought the Lord for the forgiveness of our sins, we receive rich and powerful promises from Him. ***"I sought the LORD and He answered me; He delivered me from all my fears"*** (Psalm 34:4).

It's not magic, it's faithfulness! He gives us promises to protect us and provide for our needs. ***"I love those who love me and those who seek me find me"*** (Proverbs 8:17). But we have to be students of His Word to know what the promises are and where to find them in Scripture. ***"Cast your cares on the LORD and He will sustain you; He will never let the righteous fall"*** (Psalm 55:22).

So what do we do if we are longing for security, peace, love and joy in this life as His child? It seems that we already have His unconditional love and grace. What if our hearts are longing to ***"have power, together with all the saints, to grasp how wide and long and high and deep is the love of Christ"*** (Ephesians 3:18)? How do we get a deeper relationship with our Lord so we can experience more joy, more security, more peace and experience more of His love?

"The prayer of a righteous man is powerful and effective" (James 5:16). All we have to do is ask.

When God's People Work Together

Mt. Zion Community Outreach

- FREE FOOD- Fourth Saturday of the month, 9am-Noon
- FREE DINNER- Third Thursday of the month- 5:30 pm
- Home Repair & Relief, Automotive Help
- Assistance for single moms and children
- School Ministry for needy children

Community outreach made up of
God's people in Canton, GA.

"...this work had been done with the help of our God"
Nehemiah 6:16

When God's people humble themselves, unite and listen to His voice, the impossible becomes possible. It's God's sovereign plan that His people unite with our different gifts ***"so that the body of Christ may be built up until we all reach unity in the faith and in the knowledge of the Son of God and become mature, attaining to the whole measure of the fullness of Christ"*** (Ephesians 4:12c-13). He says to His people, ***"be completely humble and gentle; be patient, bearing with one***

another in love. Make every effort to keep the unity of the Spirit through the bond of peace" (Ephesians 4:2-3).

God is glorified when we joyfully and willingly submit to His will for our lives. He wants to use His people, whom He deeply loves, to accomplish His purposes on earth. When He calls us to His service to *"rise and build"* as He chose Nehemiah to rebuild the walls of Jerusalem, we can expect opposition. Nehemiah had called on God for guidance and favor and He gave it to him. Then he went to all of God's people: ***"Jews or the priests or nobles or officials or any others who would be doing the work"*** (Nehemiah 2:16). He made a plea: ***"you see the trouble we are in, how Jerusalem lies in ruins, and its gates have been burned with fire. Come, let us build the wall of Jerusalem, and we will no longer be in disgrace***"(Nehemiah 2:17). After He told them God was favorable, they said, ***"Let us start rebuilding"*** (Nehemiah 2:18).

So, of course, opposition rose up with the construction of the walls and their enemies ***"were very much disturbed that someone had come to promote the welfare of the Israelites"*** (Nehemiah 2:10). Enemy threats continued relentlessly in several ways to intimidate them. There was a messenger who came to Nehemiah telling him to hide in the temple because someone wanted to kill him. But ***"he had been hired to intimidate me so that I would commit a sin by doing this, and then they***

would give me a bad name to discredit me" (Nehemiah 6:13).

All of God's people who were following Nehemiah's leadership persevered in unity with swords at their sides as they worked. Nehemiah told ***"the nobles, officials, and the rest of the people, 'Don't be afraid of them. Remember the Lord, who is great and awesome, and fight for your brothers, your sons and daughters, your wives and your homes'"*** (Nehemiah 4:14).

Are we getting the picture yet? This is a true account of God's people from all walks of life uniting for the glory of God. They were unstoppable. Amazingly, the wall was built in 52 days! And today, as the body of Christ unites under God, all things are possible for us, too!

Nehemiah said, ***"When all our enemies heard about this, all the surrounding nations were afraid and lost their self-confidence, because they realized that this work had been done with the help of our God"*** (Nehemiah 6:16). Then they celebrated God's goodness and greatness.

This is going on today. God's people, from different denominations, are coming together to feed the hungry, clothe the poor, counsel the needy and train those without education, through combined ministries. Our enemies are the devil, the world and our own flesh. However, when God's people humble ourselves and start serving one another in love and obedience, there is no limit to what God will do.

We are here on earth to glorify God and enjoy Him forever. Let's humble ourselves, take a good look at what gifts, talents, skills and abilities He has put in our hands, then rise and build. It's for His glory and the good of the world!

I Can't Keep Silent

Totally Devoted gathering at Salon 20, Canton, GA.
We can't keep silent!

"For Zion's sake I will not keep silent..."
(Isaiah 62:1)

My Father in heaven is blazing a new trail for me in my journey of Reading-the-Whole-Bible-in-A-Year program. Right now I'm in the book of Judges and I have tears in my eyes because my heart and mind are responding to what I have been reading. It's grievous: Total Depravity back then and Total Depravity in the here and now. And folks, I cannot keep silent. I am compelled to speak up as a child of God. What about you? ***"For Zion's sake I will not keep silent, for Jerusalem's sake I will not remain quiet, till her***

righteousness shines out like the dawn, her salvation like a blazing torch" (Isaiah 62:1-2).

I'm reading familiar verses in my daily reading but I'm seeing them in a whole new way! The LORD is opening the eyes of my heart and I am seeing two major things consistently: 1—The unfathomable love and unstoppable power of a Holy God; and 2—How horribly wicked mankind is! Make no mistake, we were created to worship GOD and our deceitful hearts lust for idols instead. I'm reading this over and over and over as I make my way through the Old Testament, and as I mentioned, I'm only in the book of Judges. That's enough for me to take in right now—but I cannot keep silent about this. I am a member of the Body of Christ which also makes me the light of the world. I am, as all of God's people are, called by my Savior to carry on His work of shining His light in this dark world.

In Judges 8, the Israelites were saved from the hands of their enemies, the Midianites, and they wanted Gideon, his son and grandson to rule over them. He was such a wise judge for the people that they wanted him as their king. Gideon told them, "***I will not rule over you, nor will my son rule over you. The LORD will rule over you"*** (Judges 8:23). He was right about that because God is sovereign and always in control of all circumstances.

However, Gideon—who was not a king—acted like a king when he asked the men to give him their golden earrings as a reward for leading them to victory over their enemies. He received about 43 pounds of gold in addition to ornaments, pendants and purple garments. ***"Gideon made the gold into an ephod of it and put it in his city, in Ophrah, his town. All Israel prostituted themselves by worshiping it there, and it became a snare to Gideon and his family"*** (Judges 8:27). In addition, Gideon's father was an idolater (Judges 6:25) and now Gideon fell into the same sin.

The study of this passage opened my eyes to how grievous idolatry is and how easily mankind falls into it. No matter how much compassion and mercy the LORD showed them as He kept forgiving and rescuing His lustful, idolatrous people, they repeatedly returned to their sin! ***"Then the Lord raised up judges, who saved them out of the hand these raiders. Yet they would not listen to their judges but prostituted themselves to other gods and worshiped them...for the LORD had compassion on them as they groaned under those who oppressed and afflicted them. But when the judge died, the people returned to ways even more corrupt than those of their fathers, following other gods and serving and worshiping them. They refused to give up their evil practices and stubborn ways"*** (Judges 2:16-19).

This looks like an addiction of idolatry! God opened my eyes to see that it is active in our present culture. We have a lusty tendency to leap back into idolatry almost as soon as God forgives us when we repent! We should not be silent about this because God offers mercy! We should be shouting this mercy from the rooftops that Almighty God promises: ***"...if my people, who are called by my name, will humble themselves and pray and seek my face and turn from their wicked ways, then I will hear from heaven and will forgive their sin and will heal their land."*** (2 Chronicles 7:14).

Our Hearts Are Liars

Lexie, Polly's personal assistant,
peering through the deck railing.

"The heart is deceitful above all things..."
Jeremiah 17:9

At the beginning of 2013 our beloved pastor strongly urged every member to faithfully read the entire Bible in one year. He even had copies available of a carefully planned year-long reading program and it was an easy-to-follow schedule printed on both sides of one sheet of paper. In addition, for those who enjoy technology, he suggested getting a cell phone app that also offered a year-long Bible reading program. He didn't want us to have any excuse for not having a schedule to follow so he also pointed us to an online reading program as well.

I don't know about the rest of the church family, but I have found this discipline very challenging to keep up with the reading program. I find that I love it. I need self-discipline. And I'm finding unexpected blessings from doing it. I'm seeing God's story in a new way. I'm being taken deeper into knowing who He is. Wow. There is no god like our God. No one.

I have not only been spiritually challenged by keeping up with the program, but God is inspiring me to write more devotions from the Old Testament, in my next book! As I'm reading the first few books of the Old Testament I keep observing that the people are so easily deceived and readily fall away from God. I'm seeing in a *new* way how awful it is that humans have the strong tendency to worship everything that isn't God. Somehow we take all the beauty that God has created and pervert it. We—our own hearts—*choose* to pervert it. They did in the Old Testament and we do today, too. Okay, maybe it's just me. But I can see it. God wants me to see this.

For example: The Garden of Eden was an actual glorious paradise of trees, flowering plants, luscious fruit trees, birds, fish, livestock, and wild animals (Genesis 1: 12, 20, 24). Then God created man in His image and gave him the privilege to name and rule over the created beings. ***"So the man gave names to all the livestock, the birds of the air and all the beasts of the field"*** (Genesis 2:20). He blessed Adam with Eve, ***"a helper suitable for him"*** (Genesis 2:18). All that beauty, all that freedom, all that peace—and only one rule: God told Adam not to eat of the tree of knowledge of good and evil, ***"for when you eat of it you will surely die"*** (Genesis 2:17). Well, if you know this story, you know that they ate the forbidden fruit and paradise was lost. Eve was deceived by the devil who told her, ***"you will become like God, knowing good and evil"*** (Genesis 3:4) and Adam fell into sin with her. Why do we give into temptation so quickly?

It's because ***"The heart is deceitful above all things..."*** (Jeremiah 17:9). Eve wanted to be like God. It's pride. It's so destructive because it's totally self-centered thinking. The Garden of Eden was a perfect place to live. It was ruined by a deceitful heart.

When Moses led the Israelites to *freedom* from torture and slavery in Egypt, they fussed and whined during their passage to a land flowing with milk and honey! Imagine. God led them with a pillar of fire by night, and a pillar of cloud by day ***“so that they could travel by day or by night”*** (Exodus 13:21). On their 40-year journey the Israelites saw God create miracles through His servant Moses with ten plagues upon the Egyptians, the crossing of the Red Sea ***“on dry ground”*** (Exodus 14:22), generously providing the perfect food for their journey, and even keeping their clothes from wearing out! How is it possible that all these spectacular things happened? It was God. And yet they decided to create a golden calf to worship and said, ***"These are your gods, O Israel, who brought you up out of Egypt"*** (Exodus 32:8). God is always faithful to His promises of provision and protection toward His people and yet we, yes, we even today, look to other gods to worship! Why? We were created by God to be worshippers. We were created to be HIS worshippers, but our hearts easily turn away. Throughout Scripture He warns His people to keep His commandments and to ***"guard your heart, for it is the wellspring of life"*** (Proverbs 4:23).

Repeatedly, throughout history, sins unashamedly rose up in people's hearts instead of the outpouring of love and worship of God. Our long-suffering God had enough rebellion and planned a devastating flood that would cover the earth. ***"Now the earth was corrupt in God's sight and was full of violence. God saw how corrupt the earth had become, for all the people on earth had corrupted their ways"*** (Genesis 6:11). Noah and his family had favor with

God because of Noah's righteousness. He and his family were the only people who were not destroyed because God instructed Noah to build an ark that would save them. We just choose not to believe God at times. Our hearts don't want to.

While we are still living on earth we will continue to have the battles of the heart. God wants our hearts to love and worship Him. This world, this culture, calls us to worship things that can be stolen, or will eventually rust or rot. Material things of this world cannot last but we seem to like to run after them. ***"All have sinned and fall short of the glory of God."*** (Romans 3:23).

There is a way to improve this heart condition of destructive pride. A healthy heart is a humble heart that lifts up the name of Jesus with great love and joy. A healthy heart is a Christ-centered heart instead of a self-centered heart. A humble heart is a heart that fully trusts God and finds rest and peace in trusting Him. ***"A heart at peace gives life to the body"*** (Proverbs 14:30). There is great freedom in having a humble heart.

Our Jericho Walls Can Come Down, Too

Totally Devoted gathering at The Soul Food Market in Historic Downtown Canton, GA.

"By faith the walls of Jericho fell..."
Hebrews 11:30

We have our own Jericho walls today and they exist to keep God out of our culture. We have worldwide walls of false religions, violent crimes, all sorts of rage, thievery, debauchery and idolatry. Then we have personal walls of dysfunction, addictions and various sinful habits. There's a dark force at work to remove all signs of Christianity from public places. Slowly the freedoms are slipping through our fingers and into the hands of people who love darkness. ***"This is the verdict: Light has come into the world, but men***

loved darkness instead of light because their deeds were evil. Everyone who does evil hates the light, and will not come into the light for fear that his deeds will be exposed" (John 3:19-20).

We are called by Jesus Christ as His followers to carry on His earthly work and obey His command: "***You are the light of the world"*** (Matthew 5:14), ***"...let your light shine before men, that they may see your good deeds and praise your Father in heaven"*** (Matthew 5:16).

God made this promise: ***"if my people who are called by my name, will humble themselves and pray and seek my face and turn from their wicked ways, then I will hear from heaven and will forgive their sins and heal their land"*** (2 Chronicles 7:14). That's absolutely awesome!

So, in light of that hopeful promise, how many Christians must be transformed into passionate, on-fire prayer warriors in order for God to heal our world? Think about it. First of all, there is a cost to become an intercessor for the glory of God and the *good* of the world. We would have to willingly give up our agendas for God's will. A life of prayer is a lot work. It is a labor of love; for Christ, for His people, and the world. He has plans and purposes for all of creation and He loves to use willing servants of the Lord to accomplish His purposes.

Joshua had faith in God and believed Him when He told him, ***"See, I have delivered***

Jericho into your hands, along with its king and its fighting men" (Joshua 6:2). All they had to do was march around the city of Jericho seven times and on the seventh day give a loud shout. God promised the city walls would collapse. Joshua did what God said and God did what He promised. Period.

Would you, fellow Christian, like to see a Spiritual Awakening in our lifetime? Would you like to witness the high and mighty walls of corrupt strongholds begin to crack and totally crumble in this world? The weapons we fight with are not physical, but spiritual. I am not describing highly-trained armed forces—not actual soldiers. I'm talking about everyday people. ***"For though we live in the world, we do not wage war as the world does. The weapons we fight with are not weapons of the world. On the contrary, they have divine power to demolish strongholds"*** (2 Corinthians 10:3-4). God tells us to be peacemakers, not violent, angry, bitter people. ***"Blessed are the peacemakers for they will be called sons of God"*** (Matthew 5:9).

So what do we do? We pray. We pray like the Bible heroes who loved God and prayed fervently to God because they knew Him and trusted His promises to His people. ***"He answered their prayers because they trusted in Him"*** (1 Chronicles 5:20). When we pray, we will get the things we are asking of God but only when they are in accordance with His will.

What do you want Jesus to do for you? Do you need a wall to come down for you? For your family? Your job? Your finances? Your neighbors? For the salvation of others? For your community? For a spiritual revival? For the restoration of relationships? For the redemption of what has been lost? What is it?

He can demolish strongholds and tear down walls of pain and regret. He can do anything.

So when we pray, do we pray prayers of faith? ***"Now faith is being sure of what we hope for and certain of what we do not see. This is what the ancients were commended for"*** (Hebrews 11:1-2). Do we believe that He is who He says He is? ***"By faith the walls of Jericho fell, after the people had marched around them for seven days"*** (Hebrews 11:30).

GOD **can** bring down our personal and even international walls. Jesus has said, ***"'with god all things are possible'"*** (Matthew 19:26). Do you believe it?

Rebellious Donkey or Thankful Sheep?

Pony waiting for trash pickup. Not a safe pasture!

"... do good; dwell in the land and enjoy safe pasture"
(Psalm 37:3b)

There is an authority greater than parents, pastors, police officers, firemen, soldiers, governors and presidents. Our parents did not come up with such rules as: *be kind, don't lie to Mommy and Daddy, don't take your friend's toys, don't hit your brother/sister*; *be polite and respectful toward others, listen to Mommy's instructions, and study diligently so you can be wise.*

When I was leading a devotion with some cheerleaders in a local high school, I said this same thing to them because it occurred to me that teenagers may think these kinds of rules originated with their own parents just to make their lives difficult!

I tried to point out to the pretty young teens those ordinances such as parents' instructions, speeding laws enforced by police officers, and safety rules firemen teach, are all biblical principles that have been harvested from the Bible!

I told them God also gave us the 10 Commandments to help us know how to live a good and godly life; in safety, in security and in love—by living according to His Word. THAT is where rules of courtesy, love, generosity, kindness, wisdom, discernment and hating evil, come from! It is God who originated, "Love Me, love others." ***"'Love the LORD your God with all your heart and with all your soul and with all your strength and with all your mind" and 'Love your neighbor as yourself'"*** (Luke 10:27). Jesus said, ***"Do this and you will live"*** (Luke 10:28b).

We, as God's people are to be faithful sheep, who remain safe in His pasture. ***"Trust in the LORD and do good; dwell in the land and enjoy safe pasture."*** (Psalm 37:3). But instead of living as faithful members of the Good Shepherd's flock, nations seem to be acting like donkeys in a safe pasture and decided to back up to a fence and has kicked the fence over with their hind legs!

So now, the predators are in our safe pastures and are devouring our unborn babies by the millions, encouraging adultery and all kinds of abominations, and most of it is coming from our own TV sets and movie theaters. And often we believe and even pay for these fantasies! I believe that there are countries that do not like God's laws even though obeying these laws produce abundant and even everlasting life. We'd rather wear masks and fake it by appearing successful and look to fleeting worldly wealth as our savior and god. I think one reason is because --as I wrote in a devotion in my first book, *It's Easier to Sin than it is to Obey, (Totally Devoted 1, pg. 86).* God's Word is true. Every bit of it. His Word has great, saving power and I know He is a merciful, redeeming, restoring Savior God. He ***"redeems your life from the pit"*** (Psalm 103:4a). He also promises that when His people turn back to Him to love and obey Him, He will ***"restore your fortunes"*** (Deuteronomy 30:3) which also means bringing back from captivity.

You see, God can fix the broken fence because He is greater than anything a rebellious donkey can do. There is more Good News, too: there is a narrow gate that leads to the Good Shepherd's safe pasture: ***"Enter through the narrow gate. For wide is the gate and broad is the road that leads to destruction, and many enter through it. But small is the gate and narrow the road that leads to life, and only a few find it."*** (Matthew 7:13-14). Our Father in heaven has given us biblical principles to live by and tells parents to ***"teach them to your***

children, talking about them when you sit at home and when you walk along the road" (Deuteronomy 11:19). And it's all for our own well-being—physically, spiritually and emotionally. What are we going to choose? Will we be a rebellious donkey and kick against the rules and safe boundaries? Or will we be a faithful sheep who is very grateful for the love and protection of the safe pasture of obedience?

We Stink!

Polly's assistant Lexie, riding shotgun.

"To one we are the smell of death; to the other, the fragrance of life."
2 Corinthians 2:16

Christian, have you ever thought of yourself as a pleasing aroma to God as Jesus was to Him? Look at this: ***"For we are to God the aroma of Christ"*** (2 Corinthians 2:15). We, and even our very lives, are a delight to our Father in heaven, just like the Old Testament sacrifices were a sweet and pleasing aroma to Him! Yes! We are ***"the fragrance of life"*** (2 Corinthians 2:16). As followers of Christ, we are commanded to daily ***"offer your bodies as living sacrifices, holy and pleasing to God—this is your spiritual act of worship"*** (Romans 12:1). This is how we glorify Him: we deny ourselves and serve Him only so that ***"through us spreads everywhere the fragrance of the knowledge of him"*** (2 Corinthians 2:14). That's the good news. The bad news is that to the ungodly, ***"we are the smell of death"*** (2 Corinthians 2:16) because we–permeating the lovely fragrance and presence of Jesus–are reminders to them that there will be a day of judgment. ***"They will be punished with everlasting destruction and shut out from the presence of the Lord and from the majesty of his power on the day he comes to be glorified in his holy people and to be marveled at among those who have believed"*** (2 Thessalonians 1: 9-10).

Have you ever been at a gathering with unbelievers and wondered why they almost seemed to be standoffish even when you were courteous? I have. Ever experienced unsaved acquaintances avoiding your invitations of hospitality because they considered you *religious folk*? Yes, I have. The truth is that spiritually speaking, we stink! We have the ***"smell of death"*** to unbelievers. Sometimes we can become such a spiritual stench to unbelievers that they persecute us. But our LORD has told us not to be ***"frightened in any way by those who oppose you. This is a sign to them that they will be destroyed, but you will be saved—and that by God"*** (Philippians 1:28).

The life of Christ and the power of the Holy Spirit in every believer cannot be hidden. We are walking around the planet carrying on Jesus' work as the light of the world! We are radiant! We have the fragrance of life! To anyone living in the darkness, we may stink; but our Father in heaven says we smell really good!

Just like the sacrifices in the Old Testament, when the priests were commanded to offer animal sacrifices of burnt offerings to God and these sacrifices were also a pleasant fragrance to Him. ***"The priest shall burn it on the wood that is on the fire on the altar. It is a burnt offering, an offering made by fire, an aroma pleasing to the LORD"*** (Leviticus 1:17). When Noah walked on dry ground again after the flood he "***built an altar to the LORD"*** (Genesis 8:20) and offered several burnt offerings of animals on the altar. ***"And when the LORD smelled the pleasing aroma,"*** He promised not to curse the ground again. (Genesis 8:21).

Jesus Christ was a glorious, holy and acceptable sacrifice to God when He willingly offered Himself as a sacrifice on the cross for the sins of His people. He is the only sacrifice that could fulfill the promise of God's forgiveness of the sins of His people. ***"Christ was sacrificed once to take away the sins of many people"*** (Hebrews 9:28). Yes! Jesus was the Ultimate Sacrifice for eternity. ***"He has appeared once for all at the end of the ages to do away with sin by the sacrifice of himself"*** (Hebrews 9:26). He carried the message of eternal life or death when He walked on the earth and it was a responsibility and privilege beyond human comprehension. Jesus is like a beautiful, priceless flask that was broken and crushed so that every drop of His fragrant perfume could be poured out to anoint each one of His followers. With the anointing of His Holy Spirit, we have a similar privilege and responsibility to carry on the message of eternal life and death. We are not worthy of such an honor but our God has blessed us with the task. ***"And who is equal to such a task? Unlike so many, we do not peddle the word of God for profit. On the contrary, in Christ we speak before God with sincerity, like men sent from God"*** (2 Corinthians 2:16-17). Just like the pleasant aroma comes from Christ, so does the power to carry on His purposes on the earth. Only His people will have the supernatural scent.

Are You Like the Others?

Radiant Sistas from the Totally Devoted weekly gathering met afterward for lunch!

"...let us not be like others..."
1 Thessalonians 5:6

When we become Christ followers, we are not supposed to blend into the ways of this world. We are commanded to stand out and shine with the radiant love and presence of God who lives inside us! ***"Let your light shine before men"*** (Matthew 5:16). We are ***"all sons of the light and sons of the day. We do not belong to the night or to the darkness. So then, let us not be like others, who are asleep, but let us be alert and self-controlled"*** (1 Thessalonians 5:5-6). Worldliness is rage, impatience, pride, senseless chatter and idolatry. It's a *Me First* attitude. Unlike the world, our walk and our talk as children of God should be filled with the fruit of the Spirit of God: ***"love, joy, peace, patience, kindness, goodness, faithfulness, gentleness and self-control"*** (Galatians 5:22-23). Jesus wants us to truly live for Him. ***"Therefore since Christ suffered in his body, arm yourselves also with the same attitude, because he who has suffered in his body is done with sin. As a result, he does not live the rest of his earthly life for evil human desires, but rather for the will of God"*** (1 Peter 4:1-2).

Nothing is hidden from God. Nothing. ***"O LORD, you have searched me and you know me. You know when I sit and when I rise; you perceive my thoughts from afar. You discern my going out and my lying down; you are familiar with all my ways"*** (Psalm 139: 1-3). That's why He uses Scripture and His Holy Spirit to speak to us! He knows we need His help to obediently follow Him. He gives us countless warnings throughout scripture about resisting evil and temptation. ***"'God opposes the proud but gives grace to the humble'. Humble yourselves, therefore, under God's mighty hand, that he may lift you up in due time. Cast all your anxiety on him because he cares for you"*** (1 Peter 5:5c-7). I think there is a very good reason that our brains are wired to operate properly when we are at peace. Ever tried to think clearly when you are anxious, angry or fretting? Uh-huh. Me, too. I can't think clearly when I'm upset. ***"Be clear minded and self-***

controlled so that you can pray" (1 Peter 4:7). Our battles are spiritual and we have a spiritual enemy. God has given us everything we need to fight back, His way. The world's way of fighting is to uncontrollably lash out with abusive words. The world's way of fighting is also to become uncontrollable in physical violence. God tells us to ***"be strong in the LORD and in his mighty power. Put on the full armor of God"*** (Ephesians 6:10-11) because our battles are ***"against the powers of this dark world and against the spiritual forces of evil in the heavenly realms"*** (Ephesians 6:12).

Our God is so loving and wise in His care for us when He warns us about sin and tells us the blessings in obeying Him. ***"Be sure of this: The wicked will not go unpunished, but those who are righteous will go free"*** (Proverbs 11:21). He promises to protect us. ***"So do not fear, for I am with you; do not be dismayed, for I am your God. I will strengthen you and help you; I will uphold you with my righteous right hand"*** (Isaiah 41:10). And tell me again, why would anyone want to be like *the others*?

Snake Stompin' Sistas

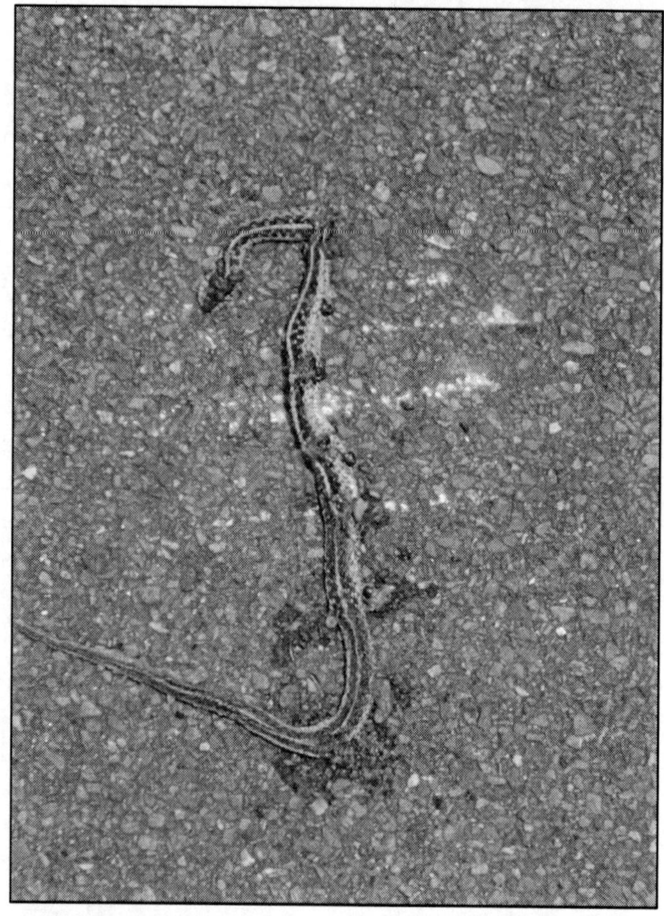

A snake that should have stayed in the tall grass!

"...authority to trample on snakes..."
Luke 10:19

When Jesus sent out the 72 to spread the Good News of the gospel He told them as His followers they had the power to spiritually ***"trample on snakes and scorpions and to overcome all the power of the enemy"*** (Luke 10:19). Today we, too have that same power with the spiritual armor of God. ***"Therefore put on the full armor of God, so that when the day of evil comes, you may be able to stand your ground, and after you have done everything to stand"*** (Ephesians 6:13).

Snakes have a bad reputation and I believe it comes from a biblical perspective. It was not a compliment to be called a snake. Or a viper. Or a serpent. I think that that perspective has not changed. Snakes are associated with all things evil. Think about this: snakes don't make noise when they are approaching. Whether they are wrapped around a tree limb overhead or making their way through tall grass, you can't hear a snake coming. This is like the devil; who is, of course, God's enemy and the enemy of His people. His spiritual attacks are subtle and manipulative. He strikes where our hearts are the most tender.

"Now the serpent was more crafty than any of the wild animals the Lord God had made" (Genesis 3:1). In fact, he was an incarnation of the devil. After he deceived Eve in the Garden of Eden, ***"The LORD God said to the serpent, "'Because you have done this, cursed are you above all the livestock and all the wild animals! You will crawl on***

your belly and you will eat dust all the days of your life'" (Genesis 3:14). In addition, God also told the serpent He would put a separation between him and the woman, and also between his offspring and hers. God promised the son of man would crush his head. This is God's foretelling of the coming of Jesus Christ who would be the One who would defeat the devil forever.

So we see that, scripturally speaking, snakes characterize deceit, evil, darkness and foolishness. Jesus said to the Jews that the devil ***"was a murderer from the beginning, not holding to the truth, for there is no truth in him. When he lies, he speaks his native language, for he is a liar and the father of lies***" (John 8:44). David prays for God to protect him from violent men who ***"make their tongues as sharp as a serpent's"*** (Psalm 140:3).

God's people are warned to ***"hate what is evil and cling to what is good***" (Romans 12:9). He tells us to not be deceived: ***"'bad company corrupts good character.' Come back to your senses as you ought, and stop sinning; for there are some who are ignorant of God—I say this to your shame"*** (1 Corinthians 15:33). I try to stay away from areas where I know snakes dwell. There are plenty that come out looking for food outside of their natural habitat. So the evil, I mean the snakes, really can be found anywhere.

However, we cannot avoid evil and flee from it if we are not alert. ***"Even from your own***

number men will arise and distort the truth in order to draw away disciples after them. So be on your guard!" (Acts 20:30-31).

I was on guard the day I decided to make my early morning workout a bike ride instead of my usual walk jog along the sidewalks in my neighborhood. Before I left our house with my bicycle I prayed, "Lord, make even my bike riding today glorify you." I decided to ride in the area behind our neighborhood where there are still a couple of farms that have not been replaced with new development. The paved road gives me a smooth ride so I can enjoy the view of the pastures, the cows and farm houses. This road is actually a back entrance into our neighborhood and I've often seen dead snakes–road kill—in the road by the farms. As I was enjoying the sunny, breezy day on my bike ride, I didn't see any dead snakes in the road but I knew that the snakes were in the tall grass. I started to get inspiration and thought that Christians should avoid the devil's territory where so many things are hidden and deceptive, too. I could see that if I enjoyed my ride staying on the paved path, it would be easy to see him coming at me and he wouldn't be able to get close enough to strike. But while I was on the right path I still needed to remained alert, and then I could resist it! I also realized that I wouldn't have a problem getting bitten by the snake unless I walked into the tall grass.

God was answering my prayer for Him to be glorified in my bike ride. He overwhelmed me with

His answer! Not only was the ride delightful but He inspired me to write this devotion! He also lovingly reminded me, ***"Submit yourselves then, to God. Resist the devil and he will flee from you"*** (James 4:7). Snake stomping is nothing more than being ***"strong in the Lord and in his mighty power!"*** (Ephesians 6:10).

Idols Are Like Weeds

Roadside stand offering luscious and bountiful fruit!

"quick to turn away"
Exodus 32:8

What is growing in the garden of our hearts? How well is each of us tending the garden of our heart that was given to us by the Master Gardener? God blesses His people with gifts and talents ***to produce fruit for His glory***. He uses scripture to teach us how to grow richly colored, beautiful gardens with the seeds of salvation He plants in our hearts. For the seed to take root, the Master Gardener has to plow up the soil to get the weeds of sins out of our hearts. He wants us to have hearts that are ***"rooted and built up in Him"*** (Colossians 2:7). Then we have the responsibility to tend our little gardens because He says, ***"above all else, guard your heart, for it is the wellspring of life"*** (Proverbs 4:23). Our Creator knows the tendency for weeds of sin can pop up at anytime if we aren't being diligent because ***"the heart is deceitful above all things***" (Jeremiah 17:9). That's what we see in the Old Testament with the Israelites who were richly blessed and cared for by God; and yet, their hearts quickly turned to idols. ***"They have been quick to turn away from what I commanded them and have made themselves an idol cast in the shape of a calf. They have bowed down to and sacrificed to it and have said, 'These are your gods, O Israel, who brought you up out of Egypt.'"*** (Exodus 32:8)

Idols are like weeds in our lives. Think about it. Weeds seem to quickly sprout up, they grow rapidly, they're hard to kill and will grow back when they aren't yanked out by the root. "When the people saw that Moses was so long in coming down from the mountain, they gathered around Aaron and said, ***"'Come, make us gods who will go before us. As for this fellow Moses who brought us up out of Egypt, we don't know what has happened to him'"*** (Exodus 32:1). Instant gratification is not a new thought! Just like people are impatient in a drive-thru line at a fast food restaurant...we make ourselves our own idols...we don't want to wait for anything. We put ourselves on the throne! As a child of God, we must yank out our weeds of sin. The Master Gardener has already cleaned up our soil. Now it's up to us to be vigilant. If our hearts are full of thorns, when we hear the ***"word, but the worries of this life and the deceitfulness of wealth choke it, making it unfruitful"*** (Matthew 13:22). Yes, craving wealth can be an idol. We must trust GOD in all circumstances. It brings Him glory!

But if our hearts have not been tilled by the Master Gardener, we have no roots of righteousness then ***"the evil one comes and snatches away what was sown in his heart"*** (Matthew 13:19).

The blessings and promises of GOD will always be fulfilled. He tells us, ***"But the one who received the seed that fell on good soil is the man who hears the word and understands it. He produces a crop, yielding a hundred, sixty or thirty times what was sown"*** (Matthew 13:23).

When the Master Gardener lives in the gardens of our hearts, He helps us tend our gardens. His desire for His children is that ***"Christ may dwell in your hearts through faith. And I pray that you, being rooted and established in love, may have power together with all the saints, to grasp how wide and long and high and deep is the love of Christ, and to know this love that surpasses knowledge—that you may be filled to the measure of all the fullness of God"*** (Ephesians 3:17-19). God helps us grow spiritual orchards!

They Turned Sweet Grapes Into Sour Whine

Polly's sweet grandnephew. He is not a Cry Baby!

"...they are stronger than we are..."
Numbers 13:31b

The LORD GOD Almighty was preparing to fulfill a promise He made to His people. He told them they were about to enter into the land "flowing with milk and honey." He told Moses to send men to explore the land of Canaan of which, the LORD said, ***"I am giving to the Israelites"*** (Numbers 13:1-2). The LORD set the stage. He told them the rich land was already theirs: they just had to take it!

These men were representatives of the tribes of Israel and were instructed to thoroughly explore the land, the inhabitants, the towns, the soil and even the fruit. (Numbers 13:17-19). The men discovered single clusters of grapes so large it took two men to carry one of the clusters. There were also pomegranates and figs.

After 40 days of exploring the land the men returned and said, ***"...it does flow with milk and honey! Here is its fruit! But the people who live there are powerful, and the cities are fortified and very large"*** (Numbers 13:27-28). Uh-Oh! Big people! Better run now while there's still time. They saw the richness of the land and the fullness of the life the LORD had prepared for them, but in their eyes the size of the inhabitants was bigger than the blessings—and even worse, they saw the inhabitants as bigger than the faithful God who sent them in to bless them. They were afraid because they looked at the circumstances instead of God. Hmm. Do we do this today? I certainly have; and when I do that I think about *myself*. That's never a good thing and it was a bad thing for them, too. When we don't believe God we lose so much.

Caleb, one of the men who explored the land, stepped up in faith and said to all the people, ***"we should go up and take possession of the land, for we can certainly do it"*** (Numbers 13:30). Wow. Such awesome, invigorating faith! Caleb had a clear vision of God's faithfulness!

But the whine was flowing freely all over the camp and the people said, ***"'We can't attack those people they are stronger than we are'. And they spread a bad report about the land they had explored*** (Numbers 13:31b-32a). And they continued to complain, ***"We seemed like grasshoppers in our own eyes, and we looked the same to them"*** (Numbers 13:33). Too much whine had blurred their eyes of faith.

Moses cried out to God on their behalf—the Cry Babies. Sorry, I just can see that if we're honest with ourselves: we are abundantly blessed people of God but we can easily become whining Cry Babies, too. Okay, maybe it's just me. But I can see it.

However, He cursed their ongoing rebellion and eventually ***"these men responsible for spreading the bad report about the land were struck down and died of a plague before the LORD"*** (Numbers 14:37). Joshua and Caleb were the only explorers who survived.

After this the people repented and said they would finally go to the new land. Moses told them ***"Do not go up, because the LORD is not with you. You will be defeated by your enemies"*** (Numbers 13:42).

To whine is a choice. Is life hard? Yes! Is there pain, heartache and suffering? Yes! Yes! Yes! But as God's people we have the privilege of using our prayers and our praises to outshine the darkness. He tells us who He is when we read our Bibles. The truth is that nothing is greater than God. He promises to never leave us. We have to keep reminding ourselves and each other of this truth. We are the Body of Christ. We are the light of the world. What if we turned our sour whine into sweet praise?

Are You An Incredible Shrinking Sista?

Shrinking Polly Balint

"He must become greater;
I must become less."
John 3:30

Anyone who is a true disciple of the Master Teacher Jesus Christ knows His classroom never closes. Nope. We are to be learning new things about Him and His Holy Word every day and

"grow in the grace and knowledge of our Lord and Savior Jesus Christ" (2 Peter 3:18). His teachings are in total opposition of what the world teaches. Jesus speaks in a spiritual sense; but the world is obsessed with the only the physical. The world teaches that a self-centered life is what makes a person great, while the Bible speaks to people's hearts with a Christ-centered focus and says ***"humility and the fear of the LORD bring wealth and honor and life"*** (Proverbs 22:4). If we are humble-spirited and faithful to follow the teachings of Jesus, we will gladly take ourselves off center stage and joyfully point others to Christ as the main attraction,: ***"your name and renown are the desire of our hearts"*** (Isaiah 26:8).

The world shouts to its citizens that to be great we have to be power hungry and that it's okay to feed ourselves on greed, manipulation and little white lies. However, scripture says our Divine Instructor must become so great in our hearts and minds that there will no longer be room for self-centeredness and deceit. ***"He must become greater; I must become less"*** (John 3:30). The world's marketing campaign is to get us to buy into the lie that if we don't enhance our appearances with non-medicinal injections and plastic surgery to help us look young, then we will not be a people of value. ***"Gray hair is a crown of splendor; it is attained by a righteous life"*** (Proverbs 16:31), meaning the elderly are honored for their wisdom, their long life for living righteously and their valuable life experiences. When God sent Samuel to find the next king of Israel He told him, ***"'the LORD does not look at the things man looks at. Man looks at the outward appearance, but the LORD looks at the heart"*** (I Samuel 16:7).

John the Baptist knew of Jesus' greatness because He knew Jesus and that He came to earth to save sinners as the Son of God! John knew ***"after me will come one who is more powerful than I, whose sandals I am not worthy to carry"*** (Matthew 3:11). One of Judah's kings, Jehoshaphat, knew of God's greatness. When he was faced with a massive enemy attack he prayed to God, ***"for we have no power to face this vast army that is attacking us. We do not know what to do, but our eyes are on you"*** (2 Chronicles 20:12). This is how we live out, ***"He must become greater; I must become less"*** (John 3:30). We acknowledge God's greatness and our total dependence on Him!

Several years ago God put it on my heart to host a county-wide women's conference. I knew I needed His help and guidance. I knew the idea was from God because I could see the path He was blazing for me to encourage women in the Lord. He had given me marketing skills, a network of Christians in the marketplace and a passion to encourage others with the word of God. But there still was so much I needed to learn! He already knew that and His Holy Spirit prompted me to memorize three verses to carry in my heart so I could faithfully follow His leadership. ***"I will instruct you and teach you in the way you should go; I will counsel you and watch over you"*** (Psalm 32:8); ***"apart from me you can do nothing"*** (John 15:15) and ***"He must become greater; I must become less"*** (John 3:30). So I understood He was saying to me; "Keep acknowledging to the world that I have given you the idea, the provision, the protection and the blessings and I will help you every step of the way. Don't make this about how great you are for doing this; make this conference about My Greatness. Give Me the glory."

Pride is sin. Pride is worldliness. Pride is our enemy. I understood. And the outcome? The local conference was richly blessed with 160 ladies, overwhelming support and provision and it was a win-win event for everyone involved. I was thrilled to give God all the glory! I learned from my Master Teacher that He is not only very great, but He is ***"the way, and the truth and the life"*** (John 14:6).

So who gets to celebrate the glorious, ultimate Graduation Day of eternal life in heaven? Yes, only His student-followers, the actual disciples of Christ who by His grace have been saved ***"through faith"*** (Ephesians 2:8). Jesus is not only LORD and Savior but He is the Ultimate Teacher who blesses His students with His greatness and His love.

"You have made known to me the path of life; you will fill me with joy in your

presence, with eternal pleasures at your right hand" (Psalm 16:11). I'm happy to be a shrinking Sista if it means bringing Him glory! How about you?

CPSIA information can be obtained at www.ICGtesting.com
Printed in the USA
LVOW13s1053150913

352468LV00001B/2/P